Winning through Cooperation

once upon a time, there was a bunch of people who were stuck in a hole

attempts were made by various individuals to get out of the hole...

...such as desperate arm flapping...

...jumping...

..meditation and levitation...

This went on for hundreds of years until they had tried everything except helping each other out...

Terry Orlick

Winning through Cooperation

Foreword by Sidney G. Lutzin

Competitive Insanity— Cooperative Alternatives

A

A Hawkins & Associates Book

Published by ACROPOLIS BOOKS, LTD., Washington, D.C.

so they helped each other out

ACROPOLIS BOOKS LTD.
Colortone Building, 2400 17th St., N.W.
Washington, D.C. 20009

Printed in the United States of America by
COLORTONE PRESS, Creative Graphics Inc.
Washington, D.C. 20009

Library of Congress Cataloging in Publication Data

Orlick, Terry.
  Winning through cooperation.

  Bibliography: p.
  Includes index.
  1. Sports—Psychological aspects. 2. Interpersonal
relations. I. Title.
GV706.4.O74   796'.01   78-6839
ISBN 0-87491-223-7
ISBN 0-87491-224-5 pbk.

Foreword

The tremendous amount of emphasis placed on competition during the developmental stages of children and teenagers is an issue of deep concern to thinking parents, teachers, coaches, and sponsors of local and national youth sports leagues, professionals in the field of leisure services, and others involved in the sound growth and rearing of young people.

The trend towards instilling the competitive spirit in boys and girls has become a primary concern among physicians, psychologists and psychiatrists. They are increasingly being called upon to deal with the deleterious effects of intensive youth competition.

The current awareness of the critical nature of the issue has led to a new effort to re-evaluate the factors involved and provide alternatives designed to mitigate the harmful effects of too much competition among children and teenagers.

Dr. Terry Orlick is one of the principal advocates for de-emphasizing competitiveness. In *Winning Through Cooperation*, he recommends cooperative alternatives to the "competitive insanity" of today. His studies of other and more primitive cultures lead him to conclude that competitiveness is neither instinctive nor a necessary factor for achieving success. On the contrary, Dr. Orlick points to competitiveness as destructive of essential social values and detrimental to the innate quality of the individual.

Winning Through Cooperation provides a solid foundation for understanding the problems of youth competition, establishes an interesting, well documented study of the issues, and offers highly reasonable and acceptable alternatives.

Parents, professionals and students will find this book helpful in developing their awareness of the issue of competition as it relates to children, programs and studies.

Dr. Orlick adds this book to his list of publications relating to youth and games involving competition in his efforts to bring reasonableness and sanity to deal with the issue of competitiveness before it is completely out of hand.

Sidney G. Lutzin
Distinguished Lecturer
DEPARTMENT OF LEISURE STUDIES
University of Maryland
Former Executive Director,
National Recreation & Parks Association

CONTENTS

The Need for an Alternative

QUALITY OF LIFE

L ast night I watched the news. I saw nothing out of the ordinary—another assassination attempt on a President's life; people tied up and mercilessly shot through the head, another series of bombs blast their way to human destruction. The places change but the name of the game remains the same.

The daily news reports are frightening exposes of man's inhumanity to man. Almost daily we see wars, bombings, killings, hijackings, kidnappings, assassinations, muggings, rapes, and a host of other examples of man's ruthless exploitation of his fellow man.

It has been estimated that 59 million human beings were killed in wars or peacetime crimes between 1890 and 1945. That's almost three times the entire population of Canada. Throughout the world, $7800 is spent every year to train and equip each soldier, while only $200 is budgeted to educate each child. The equivalent of fifteen tons of TNT is stockpiled for every man, woman and child. We have created weapons of destruction that boggle the imagination— nuclear warheads, napalm, nerve gas, lazar deathrays, special undetectable poisons. At the same time that enormous sums have been poured into military research, very little money or effort has been invested in peace research.

In the United States, a violent crime occurs every 48 seconds. In the city of Baltimore one out of every 40 people is the victim of a violent crime every year. At the 1975 murder rate, more than one out of every 200 Americans will be murdered during the course of a normal lifespan. Since 1970 there has been a steady and rapid rise in the number of forcible rapes and the chances of a Los Angeles woman being raped is better than one in ten.

Crime rates for youngsters aged 10 to 14, and for women, have risen dramatically in the past few years. Between 1963 and 1973 Canadian murder rates increased five times as quickly as the population, and incidences of assault and rape increased ten times faster than the population. In addition, the multitude of white collar and corporate crimes, in which people are deceived and cheated, most often go undetected or ignored.

Fortunately there are also countless cooperative interactions which occur regularly, in what, at times, appears to be a ruthless cutthroat jungle. Man does show his capacity to be a warm, loving, compassionate creature, in spite of having been raised in a highly industrialized and competitive culture. We each know examples within our own experiences. Numerous illustrations exist that show man's warm hospitality and tender concern for his fellow man, particularly in times of distress. We know of countless personal sacrifices for loved ones. It is this great capacity for cooperation and compassion for one another which must be nurtured, rather than destroyed. Each of us would feel more fulfilled and would profit considerably if we could both exhibit and be the recipient of humane acts such as these.

Our quality of life can be enriched by people who are warm and generous in the same way that it can be impoverished by those who are ruthless and cold. Other people trigger our happiness or misery. It is those people with whom we come in contact every day, at work, at home, on the road, on vacation, anywhere, anytime, who can make us feel good or miserable.

Our happiness and our feelings of well being are so closely linked to what others do, or do not do, that we can no longer be concerned only with ourselves. It is in our own individual and collective best interest to help others become more positive, considerate and cooperative. Think of what makes you feel really good, what makes you feel accepted and appreciative of other people—a simple gesture of friendship, a compliment or two, an unsought word of kindness, some genuine concern expressed for you. Isn't it wonderful when someone goes out of their way to help you, or to make you feel accepted, when there is no obvious payoff for them? Think of how beautiful life would be if each day the number of compassionate acts were increased a thousand fold and the number of destructive acts decreased a thousand fold.

Imagine what it might be like if, for even one day, everyone with whom you came in contact was pleasant, honest and concerned with your best interests. What would it feel like if you could always believe what politicians or government officials said; or if you could really trust a salesman; or if you could walk down the street and know that no one would harm you; or if all waitresses, secretaries and operators treated you pleasantly, not as if they were doing you a favor by "serving" you, and if you treated them in the same manner, not as if they were slaves; or if all your neighbors were consistently kind and considerate toward you and your family?

WHY BOTHER?

I am sure that every individual who has been committed to positive change within society has asked, *why bother?* Will it really make any difference? I often wonder if I am not wasting my time putting these words down on paper. But what keeps me going is the ocean of destruction that I see around me and my recognition of the positive potential of man.

In addition, a short visit to New Jersey recently was enough to remove any doubts as to whether there was a reason "to bother." During one week several ghastly events occured. A friend who just begun teaching elementary school was stabbed and stomped for no apparent reason, while working at a carnival in Newark. When I attempted to find him at the hospital, the nurses went through some deliberation deciding which stab victim he was. "He wasn't the first one." "I don't think he was the fourth." "Maybe he was the second one," that came in that night, they murmured. After four hours of surgery, the doctor said that they had come very close to losing him. The knife had pierced his lung and the bottom of his heart.

The next day, when the crime was reported to the local police, the officers mentioned that they have 10 to 15 stabbings or shootings every night in their precinct alone. They said, "It's a real jungle out there," and added that there wasn't much chance of finding out who did it. The people who live in that area are afraid to open their doors or venture out after dark for fear of being stabbed, raped or mugged. They're not safe in the day either. A teenage girl was raped and beaten to death in broad daylight in a busy section of the city.

That same week, a man was released from prison on a weekend pass and threw his two young children off the fourth story of a building. He had been jailed originally for having thrown them off the third story. All the animals at a baby zoo in upstate New York were stabbed or beaten to death. Human scavengers combed the wreckage of one of the worst air disasters in history for souvenirs, money or anything else they could find. Elderly people living in one-room slums in downtown New York told of their fear of sleeping at night, of their endless battle with cockroaches and rats, of their futile battle with their landlord who had turned off their heat and water. One of the men had been mugged five times in the last year.

And one of my close friends, who teaches in an inner city school, told me, "There's no peace here, it's just one confrontation after another." He spoke of a teacher who was attacked and beaten by fourth grade students, of an epidemic of venereal disease in elementary school, and of a third grade student who stabbed another student in school.

This inhuman jungle is sweeping out of the cities into the suburbs, out of the suburbs into the countryside, out of disturbed societies into serene societies. If we do not halt this movement we will be rapidly swallowed by competitive insanity and life will not be worth living.

Corruption and distortion of human values exists at

all levels, in all domains—in politics, law, business, sports. The competitive *win* ethic has become so intense that it is threatening to destroy our society. Millions of little "Watergates" happen every day in the name of victory.

The tragedy is that the *wins* of Watergate, Vietnam, etc., represent very serious losses to society. When large numbers of people become deceitful, conniving and exploitative, all of us are affected. If not financially, then certainly we are affected with respect to quality of life and psychological peace. When major decisions within a society are based on material rather than human profit, it is not surprising that we are moving in a direction away from human values. We cannot even hope for a decent quality of life in the future unless this trend is reversed.

I have lived half my life in the United States and the other half in Canada. I saw a serious decline in many of our most precious values and ideals in the United States and am beginning to see the same values declining in Canada.

Ironically, people are being destroyed by an extension of their own competitive ethic. They know their game of football, their game of politics, their game of life. Win in any way you can. The wholesale subscription to this principle motivates the most "savage" acts of our time. Assassins, terrorists, warriors, and war makers are not "crazy," they have merely brought the *win-at-all-costs* dictum wholeheartedly.

Most of our values are declining because people are being rewarded socially, politically or materially for their inhumanity to their fellow man. The child who cheats, the lawyer who misleads, the politician who deceives, the corporation that misrepresents, the terrorist who kills, all have something to gain in the short run. Often it is at the expense of others.

Perhaps we should no longer ask what kind of environment is producing such a twisted sense of values, but instead, we should ask what kind of environment could untwist them and would not allow them to become warped in the first place. Each time something barbaric occurs, each time the potential for human destruction and corruption is strengthened, each time the incidence of violent crime increases (which is daily), I feel more obligated and more committed to try to do something.

To merely attempt to jail or kill offenders *after* the act will not solve our problems. We cannot possibly police everyone and everything in society. We must therefore work to change the value system so that people control their own behaviors and begin to see themselves as cooperative members of the family of man. To change our environment so that corrupt and destructive people can never again exist, will solve our major problems for today and many for tomorrow.

I have gained a substantial amount of knowledge about psychological and social development, particularly as it occurs through the realm of play and games. It is my hope to draw upon this knowledge in an attempt to provide some rationale and mechanisms for positive change within our society. Perhaps if some of our most destructive adults today had as young children been exposed to the warmth, acceptance and human values which I am attempting to promote through cooperative play and games, they would have grown in another direction. If other aspects of their environment had also supported a more positive orientation toward human life, they would have acquired alternative, more positive ways of relating to people and problems. As people become more sensitive to others' feelings and more willing to cooperate for the collective good, our planet will become a much healthier and happier place to live, for all of us. Moves in this direction are absolutely essential to ensure a decent quality of life, and to ensure life itself.

For those who feel that nothing can be done or nothing need be done, Erich Fromm has an important message. He maintains that pessimism functions largely to protect the pessimists from any inner demand to do something, by protecting the idea that nothing can be done. On the other hand, the optimists defend themselves against the same inner demand by persuading themselves that everything is moving in the right direction anyway, therefore nothing needs to be done. The position Fromm holds is one of rational faith in man's capacity to extricate himself from what seems to be the fatal web of circumstances that he has created. As will become clear by reading this book, we have both the knowledge and capacity to effect positive change. All we need is the collective motivation to act.

Considering the direction in which we have been moving, and the direction in which we need to move, the statement made by Robert Kennedy shortly before his assassination has special relevance for our society: All that is necessary for the forces of evil to win in the world, is for enough good men to do nothing. This is why I have chosen to bother.

Fit To Cooperate

Competition is often thought to be "natural," "inherited," "a primitive instinct," "essential for human survival." To support these beliefs people often refer to survival of the fittest, to man's natural affinity toward competition, and to the primitive savages of years gone by. But, is competition really "natural?" Does it help our chances for survival? Does it increase the quality of our lives?

PRIMITIVE SAVAGES

In the late 1960's a lone hunter first stumbled upon these primitive cave dwellers, by accident, while wandering through a Philippine rain forest. At that time the Tasaday had no enemies and no weapons. They did not kill animals, and had no words for such things as fighting, enemy, hate, or war.

Elizalde, the second outsider ever to visit the Tasaday, commented, "These are incredible people. We can learn from them. They are simple, absolutely honest people who have found a way to live happily in their environment . . . no greed, no selfishness. Everyone goes around talking about people being bad because that's human nature. Well, I say that is crap. When you see these people you have to say, 'No, man is not basically evil.' . . . There's no greed. They share everything. If everybody doesn't eat they aren't happy . . . . They seem to forget themselves as individuals and when they look forward, they look forward together, and they love things together. . . . They are natural conservationists and they are beautiful, loving people. They don't fight—that is fantastic in this age. The world is tearing itself apart, and yet these people exist in goodness."

However, the image that we conjure up when someone mentions primitive savages is some screaming, blood-thirsty, subhuman creature. Modern man is thought to have evolved from this kind of competitive, aggressive creature and therefore is presumed to have inherited some of these savage characteristics through his genes.

But a large body of evidence indicates that prehistoric men, living together as food gatherers and hunters, were characterized by a minimum of destructiveness and an optimum of cooperation and sharing. The notion that human beings evolved and survived only because of relentless, grinding competition and aggression is not supported by the facts.

Large scale destructiveness and cruelty came into existence only with increased productivity, division of labor, the formation of large surpluses, and the building of states with hierarchies and elites. Human destructiveness grew as civilization and the role of power grew. Stone Age people that survive in remote corners of the world are usually gentle and sensitive human beings with a fine ecological sense, at least until we invade them.[1]

Today, many of us equate human achievement with technological achievement. Advanced technology and material wealth has become more impressive to modern man than kindness and spiritual wealth. Progress is viewed in a very narrow sphere. How could a savage be equal to, let alone superior to, men who can fly to the moon, or men who can push a button and destroy millions of fellow human beings?

While our society revolves around production, economization and maximizing personal gains, many primitive societies do just the opposite. They give their possessions away, they admire generosity, expect hospitality, and have negative social sanctions for selfishness. Sharing is expected and the giver is generous as a matter of course. Gratitude is not expressed since it is a state of reciprocity rather than charity. They help each other, it's that basic.

Generosity and modesty are required of persons of high status in primitive cultures, and the rewards they receive revolve around the love and attention of others. One individual may be stronger or more intelligent than others but prestige will be accorded only if these qualities are put to work in the service of the group.

Most primitive hunters and agriculturalists had no opportunity to develop a passionate striving for property or envy of the "haves" because there was no private property to speak of and there were no important economic differences to cause envy. There was no basis, or reason, to exploit other human beings. "The idea of exploiting another person's physical or psychological energy for one's own purposes is absurb in a society where economically and socially there is no basis for exploitation," says Fromm in The Anatomy of Human Destructiveness.

In his book, Fromm analyzed thirty primitive cultures and categorized them on the basis of aggressiveness and peacefulness. The eight most life oriented societies (Zuni Pueblo Indians, the Mountain Arapesh, the Bathonga, the Aranda, the Semangs, the Todas, the Polar Eskimos, and the Mbutus) centered their societies around the preservation and growth of life in all its forms.

These societies are characterized by a minimum of hostility, violence or cruelty. Harsh punishment, crime, and the institution of war are absent or play an exceedingly small role. Children are treated with love and kindness. Women are generally considered to be equal to men; they are not exploited or humiliated, and there is generally a permissive and affirmative attitude toward sex. There is little competition, greed, envy, individualism, or exploitation, and there is a great deal of cooperation. A general atmosphere of trust, confidence and good humor prevails in these societies.

The six most destructive primitive tribes are characterized by interpersonal violence, destructiveness, aggression, maliciousness, and cruelty, both within the tribe and against others. The whole atmosphere of life is one of hostility, fear and tension. There is an abundance of competition, great emphasis on private property, strict hierarchies, and much warlike behavior.

Let's take closer looks at a life oriented society as well as a destructive society. For the Zuni Indians the dominant value is life and living itself, not possessions. Individuals who are aggressive, competitive and noncooperative are regarded as aberrant types. With little competition, work is essentially cooperative and hoarding is practically unknown. Great generosity is shown to others and exploitation of others is unknown. Men do not act violently, and themes of terror and danger are not cultivated in their myths or tales.

On the other hand, the Dobuans distrust everybody and treat them as possible enemies. All existence is cutthroat competition and every advantage is gained at the expense of the defeated rival. Treacherous competition, suspicion and cruelty are the means to "success." A successful man is one who has cheated another of his place. The system fosters animosity and stresses one's own gains at the expense of another's losses. Calculated murder is not uncommon. Existence appears to be a struggle where deadly antagonists are pitted against each other in a contest for the material goods of life. Sound familar?

After analyzing many different societies, the anthropologist Margaret Mead concluded that the extent to which a society will be cooperative does not depend upon the physical environment, technological development, or on the actual supply of desired goods. The social structure of the society determines whether individual members cooperate or compete against one another.

Cultures with a major emphasis upon competition tend to have a single scale of success, a valuation of property for individual ends, and a social structure which depends upon the initiative of the individual. A major societal emphasis upon cooperation corresponds with a high degree of security for the individual, a weak emphasis upon rising in status, and a social structure which does not depend upon the exercise of power over persons, says Mead.

In our own culture we are besieged with competition.

We reward winners and reject losers. Our educational system is based upon competition. We do not teach our children to love learning; we teach them to strive for high grades. We do not teach children to love sports; we teach them to win games. When sports writer Grantland Rice said, "What's important is not whether you win or lose, but how you play the game," he was not describing the dominant theme in American life, he was prescribing a cure for an overconcern with winning. From the Little League player who bursts into tears after his team loses; to the fans in the football stadium chanting, "We're number one!"; from Richard Nixon's fixation on winning another election; to the third grader who despises his classmate for superior performance on a test; "we manifest a staggering cultural obsession with victory," Eliot Aronson points out in his book, The Social Animal.

So many examples abound of man's competitiveness, rivalry and ruthless exploitation of his fellow man within our culture that many people are convinced that this is the nature of man. If one views only the present and only product-oriented industrialized societies, urban jungles, it is easy to see why this misconception exists. However, this belief is in itself dangerous as it serves to justify and strengthen the very behavior which we find repulsive. In essence what we have is a self-fulfilling prophecy: if we believe that this is the true nature of man and we expect this behavior, then we will undoubtedly get it. Yet midst all these negatives there are glimmers of what man has been and what man can be.

The fact that there are societies where competition and aggression are virtually nonexistent, as well as societies where ruthless competition and destructiveness are the norm, leads us to believe that these are learned behaviors. For example, the Semia Tribe of Malaya does not physically punish youngsters and rarely do they see any form of violence. They have no models of aggression to emulate, nor does anyone receive positive reinforcement for aggression. Murder is nonexistent. Similarly, among the Hutterites, aggressive behavior is not sanctioned and this cooperative subculture within North America is characterized by a lack of overt aggression.

Of course, even in societies and subcultures where there are numerous sanctions and models for competitive, exploitative and aggressive behavior, there are many individuals who are in fact cooperative, kind and considerate. In spite of all the violence surrounding them, they have remained nonviolent. In a society where extrinsic rewards can be gained by taking advantage of others, there remain those who are unwilling to knowingly take advantage of others. Can then competition, aggression, and exploitation be natural to man?

In reflecting on this question, we note that maximum cooperation and sharing was seen among the Greenland Eskimos when hunting was bad, when the food and fuel supply was low, and in times of famine. The threat of starvation resulted in the Eskimo people cooperating more fully. If competition was natural for man, would increased cooperation, rather than increased competition, occur even in the face of death?

The proposition that industrialized man *instinctively* competes against fellow man, and that competition is essential to human survival appears to be a self-perpetuating myth. No evidence exists of a biologically inherited urge to compete which will damage the organism if ignored, as is the case with the need to eat, drink or breathe. Human aggression is simply not necessary for human survival; if anything, it threatens human survival.

SURVIVAL OF THE FITTEST

The concept of survival of the fittest has been misused and abused to justify the principle that "might is right." However, "fittest" was not intended to mean strongest or most brutal. Darwin himself was bitter that his theory was distorted to justify corrupt business, inhuman cruelty, and warfare against the weak. Darwin's theories of natural selection were misunderstood and misrepresented to justify exploitation of the poor by the rich. Ruthless businessmen, fraudulent politicians, and ambitious citizens rationalized their own dehumanizing behaviors by referring to survival of the fittest. They helped perpetuate the win-at-all-costs myth and the idea that "losers" deserve to be crushed. In spite of the misuse of his theories, however, Charles Darwin clearly maintained that, for the human race, the highest survival value lies in intelligence, a moral sense, and social cooperation—and not in competition.

As biologists know, even at the cellular level, cooperative adaptation has most often been the most successful route to development and survival. The evolution of diverse species was largely dependent upon the development of processes that permitted many cells to live in harmony, with a minimum of stress among them, serving their own best interests by ensuring the survival of the entire complex structure. When colonies of individual cells came together to form a single cooperative community, competition was amply overcompensated by mutual assistance because each member of the group could depend on others for help. Different cells specialized, undertaking different functions, some to look after food intake and digestion, others to provide the means for respiration, locomotion and defense, still others to coordinate the activities of the entire colony. "Among the individual cells of such closely knit complex bodies, egotism and altruism became virtually synonymous; there can be no motive for competitive struggles among cells which depend upon one another and share everything, even a single life," says Hans Selye in his book, Stress Without Distress.

There is ample evidence to support the conclusion that cooperative behavior, nonaggressive behavior, and mutual aid have great survival value.

Since the beginning of one-celled organisms billions of years ago, life has usually been a blend of much cooperation and limited competition both within and between species. The drive to cooperate is "most dominant and biologically most important" in the social and biological development of all living creatures. Species survive by perfecting their ability to cooperate with others. It can fairly be said, then, that the basic law of life is cooperation.[2]

The society of man has survived because the cooperation of its members has made survival possible. Continued cooperation is perhaps more important for man than for any other species because what man does also has a direct effect on all other species. He has the capacity to enrich or destroy not only himself, but also the remainder of our natural environment.

Yet, modern man is moving further and further away from the harmonious coexistence that was so basic to his development and survival. The direction in which man is moving in western society can be likened to the development of cancer. The most characteristic feature of cancer within a human body or within a society is that it cares only for itself. It feeds on the other parts of its own host until it actually kills the host. It consequently commits biological suicide, since a cancer cell cannot live except within the body in which it started its reckless, egocentric development. Similar extremes in human selfishness and ruthless competition will ultimately destroy both the social and physical environment. Consequently, there are no advantages in our present course. Competition in its extreme forms makes losers of us all. In the long run, there will be no winners—only losers—unless we begin to move in a more cooperative and harmonious direction.

I believe that man has the capacity to engage in an enormous variety of behaviors, both competitive and cooperative, aggressive and nonaggressive. Those behaviors which become a normal part of his repertoire will be dependent largely upon social learning which takes place in a social environment. Behavior patterns flow from the values that are acquired during childhood play and games, from the models we are exposed to, and from the reinforcements that result from engaging in certain acts. In short, we are *socialized* into constructive or destructive modes of behavior.

Consequently, the environment holds the key to our future, even for those who continue to cling to the "instinct" view of competition and aggression and for those who contend there is nothing we can do to change our course. It is a well established fact that the consequences of our acts today affect what we will do tomorrow. Perhaps by moving forward from this point, "man will complete the full circle and construct a society in which no one is threatened: not the child by the parent; not the parent by the superior; no social class by another; no nation by a superpower," as Erich Fromm imagines.

A CALLING TO COOPERATE: A CONDITIONING TO COMPETE

Cooperation "is the most positive unifying force which welds together a variety of individuals with their separate interests into a collective unit," Hartmann maintained. He went on to proclaim that the strength of cooperation lies in man's reliance upon one another.

Deutsch was a more recent researcher who systematically analyzed this proposition. He assigned groups of university students to either a cooperative or competitive learning situation.

In the cooperative group, members were informed that they would be rated together as a group. In essense, all group members would receive the same grade based upon the group's performance. In the competitive situation, group members were told that each of them would be rated in comparison to other members of their own group. In this case the grade for each person within the group would be different and would be determined by one's relative contribution in solving the problem.

The results of this study indicated that cooperation, as opposed to competition, within a group leads to more coordination of efforts, more diversity in amount of contribution per members, more attentiveness to fellow members, greater productivity per time unit, better quality of product, more friendliness, more favorable evaluation of the group and its products, and a greater feeling of being liked by fellow members. As Deutsch noted:

> It seems clear that greater group or organizational productivity result when the members or subunits are cooperative rather than competitive in their interrelationships. The inter-communication of ideas, the coordination of efforts, the friendliness and pride in one's group which are basic to group harmony and effectiveness appear to be disrupted when members see themselves to be competing for mutually exclusive goals. Further, there is some indication that competitiveness produces greater personal insecurity (expectations of hostility from others) than does cooperation.

In 1951, one of the first experimental studies on the social effects of competition and cooperation with young children was conducted. Three groups of seven-year-old children were asked to paint a group mural on a long piece of paper, under both competitive and cooperative reward systems. For the cooperative mural, the children were told that if everyone painted well and if the mural was a good one, everyone would receive a prize. The children planned the general theme of the picture and the specific parts that each would paint. For the competitive mural, the same basic procedures were followed, except that the children were told that only the best painter would receive a prize.

The children were observed painting under both reward systems. Positive behavior included friendly conversation, sharing material, and helping. Negative behavior included unfriendly conversation, confiscating material for oneself, and obstructing or dominating the work of another.

Under the cooperative condition, there was much sharing of paint, the children talked and laughed freely, and commented constructively about each other's pictures. At times three or four children worked in close proximity huddled into a space hardly big enough for two, but no one seemed to mind.

Under the competitive condition, there were many more adverse comments about each other's work, and praise for another's work was notably absent.

What made these young children cooperative or competitive was primarily a function of the social situation, along with the manner in which the particular child had learned to respond to his or her environment.[3]

A classic study in the area of competition and cooperation was conducted a few years later and led to a more thorough understanding of the conditions which lead to harmony and conflict. This study involved two groups of normal, well adjusted 12-year-old boys at an isolated summer camp. Conflict was introduced by setting up a series of competitive activities, for example a games tournament, where one group was pitted against the other in games such as football, baseball and tug of war. The outcome of the competition was emphasized by awarding special prizes or privileges to the winning team. Although the games started in the spirit of good sportsmanship, as the tournament progressed this soon changed to hostility and ill will. Members of opposing teams began to call their opponents derogatory names and subsequently refused to have anything more to do with them. Name calling, shoving and scuffles between rival group members extended outside the games and became the norm in the camp. During this process of heightened conflict between groups, cooperativeness within each group became stronger, but obviously did not carry over to relations with members of the other group. Cooperation within each group was aimed solely at trying to put down or be better than the rival group.

Once hostility had reached an unhealthy level, the competitive games were eliminated. However, simply stopping the competition did not eliminate the animosity which had developed between groups. Tension and ill will had been firmly entrenched by placing children in situations of conflict. Once distrust and dislike for the other group members was solidly implanted, even normally noncompetitive activities, such as watching a movie or eating in the same dining room, served to increase, rather than decrease, conflict between the two groups. It seemed to provide an opportunity for rival groups to belittle or attack each other.

In order to reduce this hostility, an attempt was made to establish overriding goals which would appeal to both groups but which neither could achieve without assistance of the other.

One such contrived goal involved a breakdown in the camp water supply which was piped in from a mile away. The boys were informed of the problem and worked together harmoniously for the rest of the afternoon to locate and correct the problem. A similar situation occurred when the boys wanted to see a movie which necessitated that each group contribute to the rental cost of the film. The two groups got together, figured out how much each would have to contribute, chose a film by vote, and enjoyed the movie together. In another case, at a time when everyone was hungry, a truck which was going to pick up food in town would not start. The boys all worked together, pulling on a rope, in order to start the truck.

These cooperative enterprises did not immediately dispel the boys' overall hostility toward one another. At first they returned to the previously established name calling and bickering as soon as the task was completed. However, friction and conflict was gradually reduced and eventually eliminated through the introduction of a series of cooperative ventures. The harmony which developed through these joint efforts spread to virtually all areas of interaction between the boys, as had been the case with the disharmony induced by competition. Name calling and shoving matches stopped, boys from different groups sat together at the same table and interacted in a friendly way, and friendships developed with boys reporting "best friends" in the other group.

Hostility was reduced and friendships increased by placing children in situations where they were mutually dependent. By setting goals whereby cooperation was necessary in order for anyone to achieve a mutually desirable outcome, harmony was developed. The boys were engaged in cooperative means and cooperative ends. They shared the process and the product. They cooperated not to beat or to put down others, but so that every one of them would be better off. It was through this kind of interdependence that the boys finally began to cooperate spontaneously and to really like each other, regardless of what team they were on.

This pioneering study[4] supported the hypothesis that,

when one group can achieve its aims only at the expense of another group their members will become hostile toward each other, even though the groups are composed of normal, well adjusted individuals. An important revelation coming out of this research is the fact that, in the final analysis, interdependence, cooperation and harmony among children was not achieved as a result of one team or one individual being rewarded for another's defeat, but rather through common goals which were shared by all. To introduce conflicts between groups in order to create harmony within groups is neither necessary nor justified, and in terms of cooperation and harmony among mankind is counterproductive.

COOPERATIVE EXCELLENCE

One myth which has been exploded by research on cooperative learning is that competition is necessary in order for students to learn or perform well. With respect to academic performance, it has been found that children perform at least as well in cooperative as in competitive classroom settings. In fact, a series of studies has demonstrated that children from various socioeconomic classes achieve more in such areas as mathematics, vocational development and reading when they are working together with their classmates under a cooperative goal structure as compared to an individualistic or competitive one.[5]

True excellence does not depend upon competing *against* others. Albert Einstein along with many other great scholars, artists, scientists, and humanitarians achieved greatness by living up to personal standards of excellence.

Einstein was depicted by biographers as a *noncompetitive*, mild-mannered person who wouldn't hurt anyone. There are many outstanding people making significant contributions to society who could be classified as essentially cooperative, or noncompetitive. Perhaps those who make the greatest contributions are people who are motivated more by human profit than by material profit, who have come to realize that their success does not depend upon another's failure, who are capable of motivating themselves. Making a contribution or doing something well simply does not necessitate beating someone else or putting someone down. One can be extremely competent, both physically and psychologically, without ever trying to hurt or conquer another person.

Despite these factors, it is often maintained that in order to "make it" or to be "successful," you have to be a fierce competitor, the rules have to be bent. Many people seem to feel that in order to teach children to live and prosper in society they must be prepared to be competitive and to take advantage of others before they are taken advantage of.

American children have become so conditioned to competition that they compete even when the situation requires cooperation. Their drive to compete overrides self interest. It is irrational competition.

Ten-year-old children in Los Angeles participated in a series of experiments and repeatedly failed to get rewards for which they were striving because they were competing in games which required cooperation. In one experiment, both Mexican and American children were given a series of cards which allowed each child to choose the outcome for both himself and his peer. The American children often made self sacrifices solely in order to reduce the rewards of their peers. The extent to which American children were willing to do this differed markedly from Mexicans.[6]

In another experiment with younger children, a toy was given to one child and another child was allowed to decide whether the first child should keep it. The researchers concluded, "Anglo American children are not only irrationally competitive, they are almost sadistically rivalrous. Given a choice, Anglo American children took toys away from their peers in 78 per cent of the trials even when they could not keep the toys for themselves. Observing the success of their actions, some of the children gloated, 'Ha! Ha! Now you won't get a toy.'"

Studies with North American children indicate that they become increasingly competitive as they grow older. Although the intellectual capacity to respond to the need for mutual assistance increases from ages five to ten, it is not represented in experimental game situations in terms of behavior.

Studies have shown that four- and five-year-old children in both competitive and cooperative societies are basically cooperative in their response to experimental table games. However, children in competitive cultures become competitive in their responses by the ages of seven to nine years, while their counterparts in cooperative cultures remain cooperative.

Similar trends were found in research I conducted with Canadian children. Four-, five- and six-year-old children were very cooperative in their responses to active games, whereas older children became progressively more competitive. In addition, when 12- and 13-year-old children from a relatively cooperative Indian culture in the Canadian north were compared with their counterparts in southern Canada, the southern children were found to be much more competitive, even when the situation called for cooperation.

Urban children in Canada, the United States, Holland, Israel, and South Korea are all similarly competitive, whereas rural children in these same countries are more cooperative. Ten-year-old rural Mexican children are able to cooperate to get rewards which elude their competitive American urban counterparts. This tendency toward competitive solutions for everything often interferes with a child's capacity to develop adaptive, cooperative problem solving techniques. In certain situations competitiveness can be irrational and self defeating. Experience in cooperating can help overcome this irrationality in competitive children. The fact that urban children so seldom cooperate spontaneously indicates that the environment we provide for these children is void of experiences that would sensitize them to cooperating. Yet in the final analysis, whether the goal is personal excellence or harmony among men, achievement is a *we* thing, not a *me* thing.

I LIKE YOU WHEN WE COOPERATE

Controlled experiments with adults indicate that we like people who cooperate with us more than we like people who compete with us, we like people who praise us more than those who criticize us, we like people who contribute to reaching our goals more than those who do not. We like people who do favors for us and for whom we do favors, we like people who share our opinion, who listen to us and respect what we say. In fact, the single most powerful determinant of whether one person will like another is whether the feeling is reciprocated. In this respect, liking someone seems to have a snowball effect. The more people tend to like us, the more we tend to like them, and cooperation seems to be a way of getting the ball rolling.[7]

As with adults, studies with children suggest that friendly acts given are associated with friendly acts received. The friendly or hostile behavior which children receive from their peers closely reflects the behavior they send to them. Field studies have documented increases in unfriendly behavior during competitive games. When ten- to twelve-year-old boys engaged in competitive games, almost half their interactions were unfriendly, whereas when they were in noncompetitive settings, 90 percent of their interactions were friendly. In addition, in competitive game situations, friendly behavior was less likely to be reciprocated in kind. It was concluded that competitive games greatly increase the probability of unfriendly behavior.[8]

Both disturbed children and normal, well adjusted children respond similarly to unfriendliness with approximately 80 percent unfriendly responses. Disturbed children differ from normal children mainly with respect to their initiation of and response to friendly behavior. They respond to friendly gestures in an unfriendly manner about half the time, while well adjusted children rarely respond to friendly acts in an unfriendly way. Disturbed children have not learned how to respond in a friendly manner and often seem to perceive friendly acts as being unfriendly. Interestingly, during competitive games normal children appear to respond most like their disturbed counterparts. During competitive games, normal children are sometimes extremely hostile and respond in an unfriendly fashion to one-third of the friendly acts of their peers.

It is clear that competitive situations tend to foster suspicion and lack of trust, since others are not expected to act in our best interest. Mutual trust cannot develop when one individual enhances his own position either by taking advantage of another or by not adhering to the stated rules. Yet distrust breaks all bonds and increased trust is the consequence of successful cooperation.

Mutual trust is most likely to occur when people are positively oriented to each other's welfare. And the development of a positive orientation toward one another's welfare is fostered by the experience of successful cooperation. Cooperation requires trust because when one chooses to cooperate he knowingly places his fate partly in the hands of others.

Using this knowledge, prejudice can be reduced by arranging for individuals who are discriminated against and those doing the discrimination to be cooperatively linked.

For example, although war often results in cooperative action, its ends are destructive. It is simply not necessary to create enemies to create friends. It is not necessary to have war in order to have peace. This has been demonstrated in experimental studies and is also seen in the cohesiveness and cooperativeness of cultures like the Tasaday, the Bathonga and the Mountain Arapesh. Their cohesiveness is clearly a function of the internal integration of the society and is not based upon opposition to outside groups.

To better our own society and increase our quality of life, we must develop a genuine stake in each other's security and welfare. We must promote cooperative endeavors which will foster the development of a genuine desire for others to do well, rather than poorly. We must cling to the positive elements of human behavior today and nurture them for tomorrow.

All aspects of our lives do not have to be mutually interdependent. But when we do interact with others, we should do it in the most humane and empathetic way possible. Then we will all be winners, accepted by others and at peace with ourselves.

---

[1]See Fromm, Nance, Mead, Service and Leonard in bibliography.
[2]See Gorney and Montagu in bibliography.
[3]Study conducted in 1951 by Stendler, Damrin and Haines. See bibliography.
[4]Study conducted in 1956 and 1961 by Sherif, et. al. See bibliography.
[5]See Aronson, Blaney, Johnson and Johnson in bibliography.
[6]Study conducted by Nelson and Kagan in 1972. See bibliography.
[7]E. Aronson in The Social Animal. See bibliography.
[8]Study conducted by Rausch in 1965. See bibliography.

Cooperative Peoples I Have Touched

Many warm and gentle people do live and thrive in cooperative cultures. I have been particularly impressed with the Inuit (Eskimos) of the Canadian arctic and with the people of Mainland China. I have had many touching experiences while visiting these peoples, and I have, as a result, reevaluated my own value structure and that of western society. These adventures in human learning and human values have broadened my vision of what is possible in human games and human lives.

I am *not* suggesting that we cast aside our entire way of life and replace it with another. We will never be traditional Canadian Inuit or Mainland Chinese, nor am I implying that we should want to be. We can however learn much from these peoples. We *can* attempt to bring out the universal qualities of cooperation and concern for one another and therein safeguard our future.

The five-year-olds whom I observed in the arctic, in China, and in our urban cooperative socialization sessions were uniquely different; it is their humanness which was very much the same. It is precisely this humanness that all cultures, all people, can gain from. It is in this light that I present my personal views of the following cultures.

I do not claim to be an authority on the Canadian north or on Mainland China. Although I have spent countless hours observing and interviewing the people, youth and leaders in both of these cultures, I have come to recognize that there is no such thing as an "instant expert." The people are the only real experts when it comes to understanding how their society functions for them. My view of their cultures has been shaped by my short-term experiences within them.

THE ORIGINAL PEOPLE'S NORTH

I have been to the Canadian arctic on more than a dozen occasions, and am always amazed at the immensity and beauty of its land. The Northwest Territories encompasses 1.3 million square miles and are inhabited by a small group of native northerners numbering about one tenth of one percent of the total Canadian population. Sixty percent of the settlements, which are scattered throughout this vast area, have fewer than 300 residents. Over the past seven years I have spent approximately one month per year doing research in many of these settlements, which are accessible only by water or air. I have searched the qualities of the Inuit of the past and examined what remains.

The social order of the Inuit was entirely founded on the extended family which provided a large social sphere of personal security. Widespread patterns of reciprocity and sharing of food were evident. Cooperative efforts were often needed to ensure the success of a hunt. It was not uncommon for one hunter to be extremely successful while others were hard pressed to make a kill. In a capitalistic society the price of foodstuffs would have taken a marked upward shift, reflecting the principle of supply and demand. This could not have occurred in the traditional Inuit culture. "The Eskimo recognized that despite his momentary good fortune, in the near future he might be in need. Thus the best place to store one's surplus was with those currently in need. In this way he helped to assure his future security."[1]

In a similar vein, the concept of *private* property was unknown to the Inuit. Personal property consisted of things such as weapons, tools, ornaments, and clothing which were made by the individual. "These items were not private in that they did not belong to the individual himself but to his role in Eskimo society." Borrowing or sharing of personal property was a common practice. Even the land was open for use by all group members.[2]

Margaret Mead pointed out that the emphasis of "belonging" was often reversed in primitive cultures. People were perceived as belonging to the land, not the land viewed as belonging to the people.

The traditional Canadian Inuit society was organized so that a person could satisfy his own needs and those of the group by the same act. There were many benefits to be gained from cooperating (e.g., life itself and an improved quality of life) and no advantages in destroying or weakening potential contributors. Sharing was a fundamental component of life.

Sharing patterns were reflected and strengthened in Inuit play and games. It was through play and games that Eskimo children learned to carry out the same behavior patterns that they had seen in adult activities.

DISTANCE LENDS ENCHANTMENT

I have found that the further I have gone from white man's influence, the more sincere, warm and gentle the people. Once, I visited a remote settlement in the western arctic with less than 100 residents. It is situated well beyond the tree line and is serviced by a supply plane approximately once a month. For generations there were no white men in this area. About 40 years ago, a priest became a permanent fixture in the settlement and more recently a white teacher has made this settlement his home. There is still no radio, no television, no roads, and no scheduled air traffic into the settlement.

My first morning there, I got up early and walked around the settlement. The wind was howling across the frozen land and sea. Nothing moved, only the wind. The dogs were curled up in silence, half covered with snow which had blown over them during the night. A vast ocean of whiteness extended in all directions, as far as the eye could see and for thousands of miles further. Although I had been to the far north many times, this was the first time I had felt its remoteness and barrenness. I marveled at how anyone could have survived out there. The fact that the Inuit had lived in harmony in this land for so many generations is a tribute to their fantastic adaptability and the survival power of human cooperation.

I spent several days observing children playing in this settlement. Their play was spontaneous, creative and filled with laughter. The children were almost continuously smiling, giggling and laughing. They slid down a nearby hill on their backs, fronts, behinds, on an old chair with no legs, on little boxes which were attached to an old ski, and on a little wooden runner. When the wind had blown a nearby lake clean, dark blue, crystal clear ice, eight feet thick, emerged. The children ran on the ice and slid on their bellies. One boy had a small sled with a dog pulling him to and fro across the ice. Another lad was skiing on makeshift skiis behind a dog, both having a delightful time. An Indian boy I knew from another settlement used to cross country ski around his trap line, a real integration of work and play. As we walked and slid across the lake there was a great deal of linking of arms and affectionate contact among the children. Someone *always* waited for the little ones who straggled behind.

After our long playful walk, guided by all the children in the settlement, I returned to where I was boarding. A few children came in for a visit. I had one coloring book and three colored pencils. Normally two or three children would use these materials, all at the same time. They would decide who would color which picture or which part of the picture and would continuously exchange colors, with no problems and almost no verbalization. This was definitely a cooperative act which included hanging over one another's shoulders at the table.

An outsider's first inclination would be to think how nice it would be to give each child his own crayons and coloring book. Perhaps not. After this session of cooperative coloring we had a small snack, and a beautiful little Eskimo child helped me wash the dishes, while a few others offered to dry. She always called me "white man." When she finished the dishes she said, "Look my hands—white." I nodded yes, and she then asked if all people started Eskimo and "then you keep washing and get white."

The cooperative orientation of the children's play was supported by observations in a larger, neighboring Inuit settlement about 500 miles away. The free play of these children was also full of cooperation and sharing. They helped lift each other onto climbing bars, push one another on swings, share toys and wrestle together affectionately, like bear cubs. Many times children were observed holding hands or walking with their arms wrapped around each other's shoulders. Children always said, "Hi," and often asked us our names, which they generally remembered the next time we saw them. On several occasions we observed young children offering to share food or candy with their little friends, and one time a little girl on the street offered me a bite of her popsicle. A research assistant who accompanied me on this trip was quick to comment on the marked difference in the extent of cooperative behavior among these children as compared to southern Canadian children.

My short stay in the small and remote settlement was one of the highlights of my northern trip, especially an experience I had on a trap line with two Inuit hunters. These were highly skilled and knowledgeable men who love their work and their vanishing way of life. I could see it on their faces when I was in their element, and, I might add, absolutely dependent on them for survival. When we were out on their trap line, for what was a brief period of time, I got a small taste of their way of life. Arriving at one set of traps, we found that three of the four white fox which had been trapped had been eaten by a wolverine. One trapper picked up the feet in the trap, showed them to me, shrugged his shoulders, and tossed them aside. Nothing could be done about it, so he did not get upset or angry.

This adaptability to the natural environment and to events which were uncontrollable continually impressed me in the arctic. We tend to needlessly upset ourselves when things don't go our way. Here people ride with the wind. A few minutes, hours, days, or weeks don't make a big difference. Yet the white man spends a great deal of his time worrying about things which are not that important or which are not changed by worrying.

It's interesting to note that if we had gone a little to the west of the settlement, we'd find caribou. There was a big herd out there slowly moving east. There were enough caribou within a few miles to last for the whole year. But since they already had enough meat, several carcasses each, we didn't go in that direction. We went the other way.

The white man massacred *all* the buffalo. Our original people, following traditional ideals, took one when they needed one. This was partially a reflection of different hunting methods, different perspectives on killing, but most of all a different philosophy of life.

WHAT IS ACHIEVEMENT?

The whole area of achievement is a perplexing one which I thought about a great deal while in the north. Industrialized man seems to view achievement as admirable regardless of what is achieved. It could be killing the most, receiving the most penalties, or swallowing the most eggs in a single sitting. Perhaps, as reflected by primitive man, achievement is only admirable when its cause is admirable. In some cases nonachievement may be the most admirable achievement. For example, killing only two buffalo is more admirable than wiping out a whole species.

Achievement oriented people in western culture

seem to be conditioned toward more "achievement" than is necessary. Yet one can stalk and hunt and perform many skills with great precision and excellence without being excessive. The combination of fixation on achievement and materialism seems to lead to excessive exploitation of land, animals, brothers and sisters, as well as self.

The decline in concern for our natural environment has been accompanied by a decline in concern for our fellow man. Both appear to grow out of the same exploitative philosophy. Yet to want more and more is to have less and less in the end. To be able to say: that's enough, that's all we need, is an admirable quality of traditionally oriented native people.

It is ironic that the present orientation of primitive people preserves the future while our future orientation often destroys not only the present but any chances for a long-term future. Many of our "achievers" live only for their personal and monetary future, abandoning the present. They also abandon their responsibility for the future by contributing to the destruction of the natural and human resources in their path. They are so caught up in their visions of the future that they often postpone living their daily life until death; in the process, they've contributed to the death of life.

Native northerners often refer to white men as "how much, how many" men. From their view, all the white man seems to be concerned with is, "how much is this, how many of that." We are a society fixated on numbers, in government, in research, in consultation, in business, in sales, in sports, in education, and in war. We are often more concerned with how many calls, points, or hits are made than whether anyone is actually helped or given a needed service. Numbers seem to justify programs and financing, whereas the original reason for programs existing— legitimate service to our fellow man—is forgotten along the way. Evaluation is based on externals rather than internal qualities.

However, many northerners believe that when it comes down to actually improving life, when it comes down to the crunch, all the white man does is talk. Northerners think we are extremely efficient at verbalizing but equally reluctant to act, particularly on another's behalf. We can go to all kinds of conferences, gain all kinds of knowledge, yet still we *do* nothing. Contrarily, it had been the tradition of our original people to "do," rather than merely to talk about doing. Indigenous leadership is still respected for personally *doing* something, for sharing, and for humility.

Eskimo and Indian cross country skiers who have excelled at the national and international level are careful not to put themselves above their peers, as this would certainly bring on rejection. By remaining humble and sharing their victories with the people, they take quiet satisfaction in their accomplishments, much as the great hunters of years gone by. As long as they remain representatives of their people, not solely of themselves, they are accepted, respected, and are a great a source of pride.

When competitive cross country skiing was first introduced in the north in the mid-1960's, some of the fastest skiers reportedly waited for the others to catch up before moving across the finish line. Several years later, one skier said to me, "If he [a top skier] wins, we all have done it.

If he wants to go up high, he wants all of us to go up with him." They clearly saw an appropriate way to achieve, involving sharing the victory, humbleness, and not placing oneself above others.

A BEAUTIFUL PEOPLE ARE DYING

Sadly, what has been most evident from my many northern voyages is that Canada's people of the land have been invaded by a competitive and insensitive group from another age. Only remnants remain of their rich traditions from the past.

What is happening to the people of the north is in many ways tragic but will probably go down in history as merely the price of "progress," whatever that may be. Traditionally the original people were completely self sufficient and self reliant, living off the land in what was the most harsh of all environments—the Canadian arctic. The lessons of life and survival were learned through life itself. Today, native northerners are almost totally dependent on the outside world for survival. They have lost, or are in the process of losing, many of their most precious possessions: their land, their heritage, their language, their culture, their children, their names and games.

Although few white men know much about the feelings or culture of native northerners, white men have been directly or indirectly responsible for their destiny. Neither church, nor state, nor private business can deny its impact. Children have been taken away from their settlement homes and sent to white southern schools, with white southern teachers, white southern curriculum, and white southern books. Although there is a recent trend toward keeping the children in the settlements for a longer period of time, many children have spent and continue to spend 10 months of the year far away from home in centrally located residential schools. Besides the hardships created by being removed from one's family, school is in many ways unrelated to the lives of the children. It is unrelated to life.

Parents are being stripped of their traditionally vital role of providing food, shelter, clothing, comfort, and human warmth for their children. They no longer teach their children the essentials of survival and sustenance in their harsh environment. Both mother and father are stripped naked in their own land, only to find themselves with no purpose, no meaning, no life.

The white man is on the "progress march" and as a result the natives are losing their pride, their self respect, and their meaningful existence. The youth are in a state of transience, straddling two worlds, not really fitting into either. Unemployment is high, drinking problems are prevalent, and feelings of dignity and self worth are dwindling away. A proud people are grappling with a welfare state. A beautiful people are dying.

When we are confronted with so many problems in our own culture, it is difficult to comprehend our desire to push our way of life on other cultures. When we don't even have the answers for ourselves, how can we be so bold as to think we can direct the course of others? Instead of being so quick to transform everything in our path into our image, we should be reflecting upon the ways of others, in order to enhance our own. The Inuit people have lived in harmony with the land and each other for thousands of years. A woman from the eastern arctic spoke of the lessons passed down through the generations: "Our fathers were told by their fathers not to waste anything and to share everything. We like to live their way."

Reflecting on the old days in the north, another old woman reminisced, "Coming to a trap . . . the surprise to see what's there . . . and hunting, the outdoors, sun, birds singing, driving dogs, walking, getting wood. I'd rather do it any day. You see different things each day, never know what's in a trap. Get up when you want. You have a free feeling. Trapping in the winter and fishing in the summer. You eat the food you like. I will go back to the bush as soon as the kids grow up. They need the education. You need the piece of paper even if your work isn't better." She summed it all up when she said, "We were happy, now we're civilized. People took more pride in things before. Their house wasn't as fancy but people were much happier."

An insightful old Eskimo man from the western arctic echoed some of her thoughts when he said, "My generation smiled a lot. Kids today don't smile much anymore. They're like the white man." He went on to proclaim that the more youngsters work in white man's ways, the less they smile. I listened intently as he told me more about the old days and about his concern that the smile was being taken out of life. He spoke of how people's lives now revolve around the clock. They get up by the clock, eat by the clock, work by the clock, play by the clock, and sleep by the clock.

He spoke of his sense of freedom living on the land, "You get up when you want, you eat when you want, hunt when you want, and fish when you want. Nobody is telling you what to do. You can take your family to base camp and work from there. You have to work hard but it's satisfying and you're free. That's the importang thing." He spoke of families being closer on the land, of people working together, and of people not needing alcohol when they were in the bush. Apparently they had enough stimulation and meaning without it. Life on the land was by no means easy, but it was meaningful.

As I listened to his perceptive thoughts, I reflected on some things Zuk[3] has said about how native people had practiced sensitivity training in psychology, for ages. "Their awareness of the environment, their amazing nonverbal communication, is in a sense a result of sensitivity training."

My mind wandered to thoughts about quality of life. Perhaps a good measure of quality of life would be how many times you smile (inwardly or outwardly) in a day, in a week, in a month, in a year. Ideally we should smile in work and play. Not to smile in life is to miss life's fruit, life's meaning. When a particular orientation towards life takes all the smiles out of life, is it not self destructive?

Clearly people can be extremely knowledgeable and competent without eliminating the playful part of life. Does work have to be meaningless monotony? Does it have to overwhelm our entire existence? Native northerners who follow old traditions work to live, they do not live to work. That is an essential difference.

In speaking about the future, a representative of the Inuit people said, "Everything depends on whether native people are going to be able to participate. Token participation is not enough. Control of government is not in their hands nor is any other facet of life in the north." In the words of a young Indian woman, "We need human people, not experts. We'd like to see people just being honest."

Unfortunately, honesty, sincerity and empathy are not among the virtues necessary for leadership in the white world. This is one of the main problems facing northerners and southerners alike. The people of the north have the added frustrations of trying to mobilize original people to act on their own behalf, to revitalize their own traditions, to protect themselves against absolute invasion and subsequent cultural suicide.

Many difficulties exist in fusing past and future but a basic problem today seems to revolve around the fact that there are material riches in the north, and the white entrepreneurs are determined to get them, even if it means destroying everything along the way, including the people. Competition and exploitation have created wounds which only cooperation and empathy can begin to heal.

THE PEOPLE'S CHINA

I was a member of one of the first groups from the western world to visit Mainland China when the doors opened again to westerners after the revolution. In 1972, I spent a month inside China visiting educational and sports centers, communes and hospitals with a group of Canadian physical educators.

Three years later, Patti Yeomans, who had been working with me on the development of cooperative games, visited Mainland China, armed with a host of additional questions relating to child development and cooperative learning. I also had the unique opportunity to talk extensively with two of the first groups of students to leave Mainland China to study in Canada.

I was intrigued by many aspects of Chinese society and I want to share some of my impressions with you. I hope that you will accept my comments in the positive light in which they have been written. Although I do not commend all components of the Chinese culture, I think the basic values of participation, cooperation and active helpfulness which I witnessed in China are admirable goals anywhere in the world.

VISIONS OF CHINA

I had just returned from two weeks of research in the MacKenzie Delta area of the western arctic and the next thing I knew we were flying to Hong Kong. After spending the evening in Hong Kong, we boarded a train for the People's Republic. I got off the train and walked across the border full of wonder and uncertainty. What will it be like, how will we be received? I was excited and wanted to experience the culture and the people to the fullest. I wanted to be as open as possible to their way of being and to learn as much as was humanly possible in a period of one month. It was to be a month of intensive involvement. I watched closely, I listened attentively, I asked thousands of questions. I participated, I played, I exchanged points of view, I touched the people and they touched me.

Contrary to the stereotype of the outside world, I found the Chinese people, about 80 percent of whom live on agricultural communes dotted across the countryside, to be warm and compassionate individuals. Their curious faces were transformed to smiles with the slightest gesture of friendship on our part. I felt that the people had a sense of meaning, a sense of purpose, which I had not witnessed before and have not witnessed since. It was like one big family all working together to better itself. The traditional extended family appeared to have been strengthened and broadened to include an entire people. A humanness was evident that I had never expected to find.

I could not help feeling the warmth of the people. I could not avoid being impressed by the value structures of honesty, self sufficiency, cooperation, and concern for others. I could not help being impressed by the tremendous strides made toward equality between men and women. I was overwhelmed by seeing the worth of man and woman being judged solely by his or her contribution rather than by material possessions.

The Chinese are rich in ideology and concern for their fellow men and relatively poor, by western standards, in material possessions. However, when a society values man for nonmaterial possessions, who needs materials beyond basics? How much money or luxury do we really need to have happy and fulfilled lives? The security of belonging and the feeling of being needed are most important.

Knowledgeable people in China indicated that there were very few psychological problems among the Chinese people and very little crime. This may be attributed to their sense of purpose and their commitment to work in the service of some cause that they respect. China is a land of total employment, of active citizen participation in health care, in sports, in work, and in play. Chinese youth devote time to the community by doing such things as planting, harvesting, building, and there is a meaningful place for older citizens. People of all ages with whom we came in contact during scheduled events, and, more importantly, during spontaneous encounters, seemed to be happy, socially involved people. They were proud of the progress they had made and, although humble, were not reluctant to point this out.

CHILDREN IN CHINA

Of everything I witnessed in China, I was most impressed with the young children. They seemed amazingly self assured and self disciplined. They demonstrated a concern for one another which is rare in other cultures.

I will attempt to outline the socialization process which children undergo. They are taught to love and care for each other, and to be responsible human beings.

The major objectives of "The East Is Red" nursery school/kindergarten in Kwangchow are to teach the children to help each other, to take care of each other, to work hard, to keep fit, and to learn from the peasants and workers. The head of the school said that they use a positive approach in their teaching, rather than punishment.

One kindergarten lesson we observed began with praise for Dr. Bethune, the Canadian doctor, who unselfishly helped the people of China. This was a lead-in to a lesson on cooperation. At the front of the room were a series of pictures of children helping other children and children helping older people. The children were asked to tell a story about what was happening in the pictures. One child would go to the front of the class and tell a story about one picture. After he finished all the other children would clap and another child would then focus on the next picture and add to the story. The picture story we heard was about how children helped an old lady who fell down and dropped her parcels. After this story had been completed, the children were asked to tell of their own experiences of being helped or of helping people. One little boy said that he had ripped his paper and another child gave him a new piece. All the children applauded.

There were several pictures and posters on the walls, showing children sharing and helping each other. The models in the pictures were always the size of the people in the setting and always included both boys and girls. One such picture showed a little girl combing another girl's hair. The caption read, "It's good to help each other."

I bought a children's book in Peking called *I Am On Duty Today*. It is a story about nursery school children who take turns helping to run the nursery. They go (in pairs) to classroom early and do their work "happily." Some excerpts from the book are outlined below:

> I am on duty today, helping in our nursery . . .
> First, Tung-Tung helps me move the table. Then we arrange the chairs. We tidy the book shelf and put the toys in order.
> I change the water in the gold-fish bowl, Tung-Tung goes to look at the sunflowers . . .
> Now our little friends arrive. "Good morning." "Good morning, everyone."
> Show me your hands, both back and front. . . . This job must be carefully done, for we care about cleanliness, though we are small. . . .
> We stretch up high and bend down low. One, two; one, two; one, two. How well we keep together! Exercising every day keeps us healthy.
> Teacher rings the bell, ding-dong. And now our class begins. "Sit down quickly little friends. Be quiet and don't make a noise."
> I give out the pencils, Tung-Tung passes round

the paper. We learn our numbers, then we write, listening carefully to the teacher.

Tung-Tung and I put out the little bowls and fill them with rice. . . . After dinner we make the beds, and the children lie down to rest. When the others are tucked in, I go to sleep. After our nap we have refreshments. Tung-Tung passes the sweets and I take round the biscuits. The large and good ones I give to other children, and keep the small ones for myself.

We take good care of the toys we share, rocking our wooden horses gently. If anyone falls, I go to help them.

And now we tidy the tables and chairs
and put away the books and toys
all in order, for tomorrow
So our friends on duty will have no trouble.

Our teacher praises us and says, "You have done very well."

Chinese nursery school children learn to button their own clothing but also learn to button other children's clothing; children take turns pulling each other in little wagons; children pass shovels back and forth. Throwing sand is unheard of (it would be an infringement of others' rights); children play with dolls of both sexes; and children frequently take walks together hand in hand or arm in arm. Nursery school children sit across from each other stringing beads from opposite ends of the same string. Teachers encourage young children to help a classmate who has fallen down, preschool children help each other with their winter jackets, which button up the back. I observed kindergarten children learning to plant seeds and pull weeds in shared garden plots; swings built for two children or for small groups of children, and wooden rocking horses on which two, three or four children could play. Two children also shared a double sized desk in classroom setting.

Children are tied into the society and are made to feel important at a very early age. They are told, and are made to feel, that their contributions are important and are encouraged to help each other. This was evidenced by eight-year-olds learning how to cut each other's hair, by third, fourth and fifth grade students making wooden toys for kindergarten and nursery school children, and by older children conducting puppet shows for younger children. Elementary school children were taught applied skills such as gardening or acupuncture, which they practice on one another.

A portion of the school day is devoted to factory work which is nonexistent in the western educational system. In one kindergarten class children spend about twenty minutes a day taking the cork out of bottle caps or folding up padlock boxes for the local factory. The children are told that they play an important role in bettering the society and that their work helps the country. With the bottle caps they also learn about recycling materials. In addition, the school gets books and other supplies in exchange for the work done for the factory, so that it is not just an exercise. It has a definite purpose. Young children are expected to be helpful and to learn such things as acupuncture techniques. It's all very "natural."

I observed a great deal of physical contact among children and a complete absence of physical aggression. Older children often hold hands with younger children or carry babies. Mothers have their babies strapped to their backs. Young children are taught to take care of each other and older children not only take care of each other but are also taught that they should "take more care of younger children." Children of different ages are linked together by this behavior. Peers are recognized as having great importance in the socialization process and are tied into the teaching process at a very early age. They are an integral part of the process of behavior acquisition and behavior change.

On several occasions the question of how to handle "problem" children was raised. Although there are apparently very few problem children, they seem to be dealt with in the following manner: First, the teacher will talk to the whole class to explain how important it is for everyone to do his share, why it is wrong to behave in a certain manner, and what is a more appropriate way of behaving. If after doing this the problem still persists, the other children in the class will either help on their own accord or will be asked to help. The children will be told that they should always help each other and learn from each other. The parents may also be asked to help. Chin-Chin, an elementary school student who had taken part in helping with this "reeducation process" said that at first he and the others were always telling the "problem" student how lazy he was and how he was not helping the Chinese people. Chin-Chin went on to say that it wasn't until later that he and his classmates realized that they were trying to help in the wrong way. "A more positive approach should be used," he said. So they not only began to praise their classmate when he behaved well, but also encouraged him, helped him, and commended him *if* he applied himself. This reportedly resulted in a marked improvement in social behavior and school performance for the "problem" student.

If an individual is not doing well, the Chinese feel that

it is up to everyone to help that person. It is a collective responsibility to help another deal with obstacles. Students from Mainland China studying at the University of Ottawa told me that if a child is "naughty," other children will generally talk to him, help him, and explain the importance of cooperating, without the teacher having to say anything.

Role playing, singing and dancing have a major role in young children's activity programs. Children do a great deal of role playing about working together and helping others. The major values of the society are dealt with in this manner in nursery school and kindergarten. In one case a role playing incident involved a ping pong game where one child was supposedly hurt. The imaginary game immediately stopped at this point and one child moved to assist the other. The objective was for children to learn that friendship and concern for others comes first; competition comes second.

Puppet shows are another medium used to promote cooperation in games and in day-to-day living. On one occasion a group of older elementary school children came in to do a puppet show for nursery school children, ages three to five years. When the curtain opened one young puppet was playing alone with a colorful new ball. He said that he didn't like playing by himself and that he wanted to share his ball with his friends. He went looking for his friends. When he found them, they played with each other, passing the ball back and forth and had a delightful time together.

Mass demonstrations in stadiums, along with sports days held on school fields across the country are monuments of participation and cooperation. Six hundred children in teams of thirty can be doing symmetrical gymnastic stunts or pyramids which form a pattern covering an entire field.

As many as 1500 children, linked together in teams of 100, can be seen weaving up and down like a gigantic wave. Gymnastic demonstrations in China generally include an acrobatic routine where four people work as a unit doing a series of stunts and balancing maneuvers. Another event which is often included is the original Chinese art of wu shu, or Chinese boxing. Generally two, three or four participants thrust arms, legs, or sticks toward one another, barely missing because of last second ducking, rolling and jumping. The participants go through these routines with great speed and precision.

Even during the morning exercises done at school, an entire elementary school body will move out of the school, into the playground area, and form precise lines in a matter of a few minutes. Students direct one another and lead the exercises which are done to music. Pushing, shoving, goofing-off are rarely (if ever) seen.

SOCIALIZATION IN CHINA

One of the greatest lessons of China for me was seeing the incredible strength of the socialization process. While in China, I became aware of the many ways in which the Chinese try to promote their basic ideology of cooperation and working for the good of the people. Almost everything in China has some educational purpose. A similar message comes through comic books, children's books, children's plays, puppet shows, feature and documentary films, theatre, music, exhibitions, art, sculpture, woodcuts, pictures, posters, stamps, billboards, dances, songs, physical culture, school, industrial work, agricultural work, historical sites, ballets, and even the circus. Even the rent collection courtyard displays accomplished sculptures of oppression and of the peasants' subsequent revolt. The Forbidden Palace is a living monument of how the emperors lived while the peasants starved. The large pictorial billboards in the streets almost always show men, women and children all working together toward common goals.

On the other hand, the only "ethic" which is pumped at our people with such regularity is the message to consume, to buy, to consistently strive for more money and for bigger and better material possessions. Virtually all forms of mass communication in North America, including radio, television, magazines, newspapers, billboards, even sky writing advertisements, are prime movers in this area. Another "value" which is often learned in our schools, our games, our work, and through real life and media models, is competition used as a means for achieving personal ends. Consumption and competition are the basic messages of our society and it is difficult for us to escape them.

After seeing a few Chinese movies I asked one of our interpreters if all Chinese movies had a message similar to the ones we had been seeing. I was told that the purpose of Chinese movies is to educate. Our interpreter then asked, "What are your movies about?"

I thought for a moment and then answered, "They're about all kinds of things, robbery, sex, killing, monsters, comedy."

She asked curiously, "What is their purpose?"

I spluttered around a bit and then said, "Entertainment, I guess."

I realized that the primary purpose of movies in our

society, along with the primary purpose of many other things, is material profit.

I looked at a series of children's books in China and thought of some of our children's books at home. There is a very definite educational message in their books which is notably absent in much of the literature and cartoons directed at our children. Read a few commercial children's books, or better yet, watch Saturday morning cartoons to see if you can decipher any worthwhile message. Again I feel this is largely because decisions to publish books (or to show cartoons) in North America revolve around material profit. Nothing else really matters to either the publishing or film industry.

An author may want to get an important message across to the public and the publisher may acknowledge the value of the message, but "regretfully" reject the book, strictly for monetary reasons. Publishers often don't think the market is big enough.

Marketing decisions may also have a great deal to do with the answer to questions which were asked of me in China, which were difficult to respond to.

"How can you have poor people in such an affluent society?"

"How can you have unemployment when there are so many important things to be done?"

China is a nation with a very strict moral code. We never saw any drunks or any beggars, and from all reports premarital and extramarital sex is almost unheard of. Yet there's little in our culture that is purported to be more natural than sexual intercourse.

When we asked a group of high school teachers in

China whether sex education courses were taught, they broke out in a roar of laughter. Apparently there is absolutely no need for such a course. We then asked what happened to high school girls who got pregnant. One teacher said she had never heard of such a case in all her years and another said that he had heard of such an event occurring somewhere in China years ago. Premarital sex is apparently just not acceptable.

Using the North American culture as a baseline, the premarital sex "no-no" may be difficult to imagine. However, after gently picking away at this question with interpreters whom I had come to know quite well, and following up with university students who had left the Mainland to study in Canada, I came to believe that premarital sex was in fact uncommon. This is simply the result of differing socialization processes. Our society teaches about sexuality through advertisements, books, movies, magazines, peer pressure, and so on, while their society deals with sex in another way. I am not placing any value judgments on this, but merely point this out to further demonstrate the strength of the socialization capacity.

For example, if we consider only one's biological makeup, we might contend that for a man interested in gratifying his sexual urges, any attractive woman is an attractive woman. But is she really? In our culture it may be acceptable, stimulating, even admirable, to engage in sexual intercourse with certain people, yet the mere thought of sleeping with equally attractive people such as a sister or brother, mother or father, daughter or son, is considered to be revolting and is rejected outright. These are selectively socialized attitudes. Similarly, males have the same kind of tear ducts as do females. Yet many females in our culture often cry while males rarely cry. Why? Again it is part of our socialization process. It is acceptable for one group of people to cry, but it is not for the other. If we can effect these kinds of responses through social learning, we can certainly effect other kinds of responses.

While I was in China I saw that all the theories and studies relating to applied social learning, contingency management, modeling, and applied behavioral psychology are in practice there. The consistency with which certain behaviors are modeled and positively reinforced in all aspects of their lives is remarkable. It became evident to me that while the forerunners of behavioral psychology were busy in their labs, Mao was busy shaping a nation of 800,000,000.

Within twenty years this huge nation emerged from the devastation of war, from poverty, disenchantment, crime, and drugs in the streets—a truly remarkable accomplishment. The Chinese people have the basic ingredients for a happy and meaningful life, and there is an almost mystical or religious aura which surrounds Chairman Mao and his thoughts.

Ah, but they have no freedom, some will say. As a result of many discussions with and through our interpreters in China and further discussions with Chinese students studying here, I understood that they feel free, and perhaps even think that they are more free than we are, because others in their society are not free to infringe upon their basic rights.

I asked a young female interpreter who travelled with us whether she would rather be an English teacher or an interpreter.

She responded, "I'd rather do what I'm most needed to do . . . where I can serve best."

I continued, "But what would you really rather do if you could do either?"

Her response was, "I'd really rather serve where I'm most needed."

This may sound farfetched from our perspective but it is not when placed in the context of the socialization of that society. The rewards of the society come from serving others. You can feel good about yourself, you can feel good about contributing to others, and you can gain recognition from your helpful acts. The main criteria for advancement in school and in other endeavors revolve around positive attitudes toward the group.

An interesting incident occurred with respect to "the rights of others" when the first group of mainland Chinese students came to Ottawa to study English at Carleton University. I went to talk to the students to see how they were adjusting to our society. They were living in a dormitory and they told me they were having some trouble adjusting to the custom of playing loud music into the late hours of the night. It was difficult for them to imagine how a few individuals could play their radios and stereos so loudly when others were trying to sleep. They were too polite to say anything and wrote this off as a strange western custom. This kind of inconsiderate behavior would be unheard of in China. It simply would not be done.

Something else which amazed them was the North

American game of tackle football. They couldn't quite see the point of putting on "armor" and smashing into one another, a strange custom indeed.

GAMES AND SPORTS IN THE PEOPLES' REPUBLIC OF CHINA

In America, a professional football coach named Vince Lombardi is considered to be one of the greatest coaches of all time. He is noted (rightly or wrongly) for his statement: "Winning isn't everything, it is the only thing."

In explaining the contrasting Chinese sporting philosophy, *Friendship First, Competition Second*, the Chairman of the All China Sports Federation told me, "Winning or losing is only temporary, friendship is everlasting."

The difference in sporting emphasis between China and the United States clearly depicts the differences between the cultures. In China, sports and physical activities exist for the people. Consequently an attempt has been made to do away with "the past practice that only a few are kept busy while the majority look on." China has recognized that sports have more to offer than merely scoreboard winning. Sports have been used extensively for "building the people's health" and for promoting interpersonal relations and cooperation. They also served as the means for the initial reopening of cultural exchange with the west, sometimes called ping pong diplomacy.

Literally hundreds of millions of Chinese people, both males and females, are involved in sports, physical activities, and daily exercises. There are 4,000 volleyball teams in a single Chinese county known as Tai Shan County, "the land of volleyball." Three hundred thousand people participated in one table tennis tournament in the city of Shanghai. People of all ages, in all walks of life, exercise on a regular basis as a part of their normal daily routine. Early in the morning people do morning exercises in the schools, in the factories, in the communes, in the parks, and even in the streets. Table tennis, track and field, swimming, volleyball, and gymnastics are all engaged in by millions of people. Participation itself, at any level, is viewed as a form of success. You do not have to be the best to be a welcome participant, whether it be in sports or helping with a harvest.

Many factories and communes as well as schools in China have their own sports facilities and sports teams. The facilities are usually built by the people themselves. For example, the county seat for Fu Chen commune had recently completed an Olympic size, 50 meter pool, which was dug by the local students and peasants with picks and shovels, a monument to what can be accomplished through responsible cooperative efforts. An adjoining diving pool was in the process of being completed during our stay.

The students make and repair their school's sports equipment, including such things as gymnastic apparatus and ping pong tables. If factory workers want a basketball court, they get together and construct it. These tasks bring people together to work towards common, mutually beneficial ends. They also promote self reliance and reportedly help "to cultivate the habit of caring for public property."

We tend to use sports as a training ground for competitive and aggressive behavior. But through a different kind of emphasis, China uses sports as a training ground for cooperative and collective behavior.

Chinese athletes are very noble and honest in their approach to the game as we saw in a provincial volleyball game. Towards the end of a very closely contested game, a six-foot, nine-inch Chinese player leaped into the air and spiked the ball with great accuracy to tie the game at 14-14. After being awarded the point, on his own accord he raised his hand to indicate to the official that he had touched the net. The point was withdrawn and the crowd cheered this athlete for his honesty. In addition, officials (generally of the same age and sex as the players), have their calls accepted without dispute, and team captains always shake hands with the officials, both before and after the game.

Purposeful cheating or foul play (eg., tripping, throwing elbows, etc.) is not acceptable behavior. The emphasis is placed on honesty, cooperation and mutual help. Whenever a foul occurs in a game, the athlete who committed the foul apologizes and shakes hands with his opponent. He or she appears to be totally sincere in the apology. If a player is knocked down in a game, for example in basketball, a member of the opposing team will help him up, even in the heat of competition.

In a women's provincial volleyball game, in the midst of a rally, a girl left her area uncovered to go under the net to help an injured opponent off the floor. In another incident, near the end of a closely contested basketball game, just as a middle-school girl was taking aim at the basket, a girl on the other team, who had been following her down the court, tripped and fell. The girl preparing to shoot stopped to help her "opponent" up. When play resumed the girl who had been preparing to shoot merely put the ball back into play from the sidelines.

The University of British Columbia hockey team travelled to China in 1973 to play some Chinese teams. On one occasion, "early in the first period the spectators moved to the edge of their seats as a Canadian, tussling with a Chinese in a corner of the ice, raised his fist in a fit of momentary anger. The moment passed quickly, and as the two players skated back into the play, the Chinese patted the Canadian on the arm in a gesture of conciliation. The Canadian, apparently unfamiliar with such mannerisms on the ice, hesitated for a moment, before reciprocating with a pat on the behind. The crowd roared with approval," reported the Toronto Globe and Mail.

When the Chinese gymnasts competed in the United States one of the U.S. gymnasts had problems with her floor exercise music. The Chinese pianist accompanying the Chinese team willingly played for her, even though this was likely to increase their "opponents'" score.

When the Chinese gymnasts first came to Canada, they refused to compete. They wanted to perform together in a friendly demonstration, and they did just that. A Canadian gymnast, who was a member of that Canada-China demonstration tour, recalled her experiences with the Chinese gymnasts as a highlight of her gymnastic career. She described the Chinese girls as being "very warm and friendly."

In China a typical sports event begins by both teams chanting in unison, "Promote physical culture—build the people's health." One team then shouts, "We learn from you," to which the other team responds, "We learn from you," and then in unison, they shout, "We learn from each other." The athletes run towards one another and shake hands. The team captains shake hands with the officials and the game is ready to begin. If there is a scoreboard, Friendship First will probably be written on it.

A similar procedure is followed with young children. For example, a tug of war begins with the two "opposing" teams holding hands, waiting side by side in two lines. The children chant, "Physical culture is for the people," and run to their respective ends of the rope. They then raise their hands and say, "Friendship first, competition second." When the game is over they chant, "We learn from each other," and return inside walking hand in hand.

Darwin Semotiuk, a traveling companion in China, noted an interesting incident which occurred during a 100 meter swimming race. Once the swimmers had started the race, the spectators were silent through the first 25 meters, followed by enthusiastic cheering during the next 50 meters, and then silence again for the last 25 meters. There was no ovation or presentation to the winner. Cheering occurred again only when the last swimmer had completed the race. According to the Mainland Chinese students studying at the University of Ottawa, this is a common occurrence. "We always give applause to the last one, he has will, and is trying to catch up with the others."

While in China a Canadian physical education student wrote about her feelings about playing basketball with a group of Chinese students: "For the first time, as a mediocre player, I felt as though I belonged to a team. I didn't feel as though the other players thought I was a lousy player. The ball was always passed to me and I felt a part of the game, someone who could help out, and was not just in the way."

In China it seems to me that sports do serve people. Competition is friendly, and games are semi-cooperative. The game never becomes more important than the people. In all the games I viewed in China, at all skill levels, I never saw a temper flare, I never saw anything resembling an intentional foul, I never saw a pushing match, a shoving match, or a fight. Perhaps this is the kind of sportsmanship that used to be evident elsewhere in the world. In many of the children's games I observed, the children merely played the game and when it was over, that was it. No winners were declared, no fanfare was evident. The process seemed to be the important component.

DEPARTURE FROM THE MAINLAND

After a month of immersion in this new culture, certainly one of the greatest learning experiences of my life, the time had come to depart. Genuine tears were shed by some members on both sides at the border, for we had come to appreciate our Chinese travelling companions and they had come to know us.

Coming out of China into Hong Kong was like hitting a brick wall. Beggars, thieves, crooks, drug pushers, prostitutes, dirty streets, advertisements were plastered everywhere. Striking distinctions between rich and poor were obvious with mansions aside hole-in-the-ground shacks. Hong Kong is the western world at its worst, with everyone trying to take advantage of us with their "bargains," people trying to pick our pockets, people following us down the streets begging for money. We had to literally hang on to everything and lock everything up. In China we had never locked hotel doors and we never lost a thing. This re-entry into Hong Kong was a very depressing experience.

To top it off, four of us went to eat at the Hong Kong Hilton and were refused entry, the worth of a man being judged by the clothes on his back.

Perhaps we had come to China at an ideal time, before the borders were really opened, before white men with round eyes were again to be a common sight, before the influence of the outside world could begin to assert itself. Things in China have undoubtedly already changed somewhat. I only hope we can learn from some of her positive accomplishments.

China's big test will be her ability to draw from her most humanistic leanings despite transfers of leadership and the onslaught of the outside world. In sports the outside intrusion has already begun. At a coaching clinic in Peking, a Canadian hockey coach reportedly told the Chinese that they would have to learn to hit if they wanted to win in the world competition. The long range effect of this kind of advice and competition against outside teams cannot yet be determined. Only time will tell.

Perhaps China does have a built-in safeguard with only those who have demonstrated a concern for others rising in the system. Theoretically it should continue. However, the long standing spiritual core of cooperative leadership, Mao, has died before the first citizens who have blossomed in the New China are old enough to assume leadership. The gap between the child's early years and years of influence and leadership has not yet had time to fully close. Consequently the interference of older adults, who have been raised under another value system, may well cause some problems. If an acceptable form of positive, cooperative leadership can survive until some of the most capable, and cooperative New Chinese youth become leaders, the cooperative ethic will in all probability survive and prosper.

The reactions of the outside world to China are predictably varied. While some are excited about her development, others are very skeptical. After reading an article I had written on sports in Mainland China, one student responded, "This article is simply propaganda. I don't believe they actually believe their motto, Friendship first, competition second. They play to win. In some respects, I think the Chinese can be compared to the Nazis."

Can a person become so conditioned to one culture that he cannot open his eyes wide enough to see another? Have we moved so far from basic human values and ideals that we cannot even imagine that they could exist? Must cooperation be "a put on" or "propaganda"?

Another individual commented, "Outwardly they show these feelings of cooperation, but it is because they would be punished if they didn't."

If this point has any credence, then could not the same point be raised in an attempt to explain competition in our own culture? Outwardly we shows signs of competition but it is because we would be punished if we didn't.

Whether you believe my impressions of China are accurate or not is not that important. The important point is that we must take positive steps to introduce the kinds of values that we feel are important for our people, to ensure a decent quality of human life.

My perception of the ethic of new China—not to hurt or infringe upon the rights of others—is the kind of ethic which must transcend nations, as many people throughout the world are beginning to recognize. For all nations the preservation of human values should mark the success of a people. The ability to live in a meaningful and cooperative fashion should mark the success of man.

[1,2]*See Glassford (1970) in bibliography.*
[3]*In* "Indian and Eskimo Games," *The New Trail, 1969. See bibliography.*

Fit To Destroy

"**I** knew it was right, because it felt good when I was doing it," said Susan Atkins, a member of the Manson Family when explaining her justification for the horrible murder of seven people. When describing her part in killing Sharon Tate, a talented young actress who was eight months pregnant at the time, Atkins said, "I just stabbed her and she fell, and I stabbed her again. I don't know how many times I stabbed her. . . . Sharon begged for the life of her baby, and I told her 'shut up. I don't want to hear it.'" When questioned about her feelings towards her victims, Atkins responded, "I didn't know any of them. How could I have felt any emotion without knowing them? They didn't even look like people. . . . I didn't relate to Sharon Tate as being anything but a store mannequin. . . . She sounded like an IBM machine. . . . She kept begging and pleading and pleading and begging, and I got sick of listening to her so I stabbed her."

None of the participants in these ruthless and senseless slaughters expressed any sense of guilt or responsibility whatever, nor did they feel the slightest bit of empathy for their innocent victims. They are a prime example of "doing your own thing" gone mad.

We can only "do our own thing" constructively if we have been socialized to feel good about humanistic events. This was certainly not the case with the Manson Family. They had a history of early alienation and rejection. Their lives were barren of experiences in tender human cooperation and compassion. Their models were violent. They were created by a society which allowed them to grow in a twisted form and which they subsequently began to destroy. If nothing else, they were incredibly fit to destroy.

WHAT'S ON THE TUBE?

We have the means to do almost anything but we have no common ends. We lack a commitment to a human oriented value system. Let's look at the values promoted by television, as an example. Television has great potential for positive social development, for positive socialization, but it is rarely used this way. Instead it sells violence and materialism as a way of life. The media are certainly not the only offenders but are a major contributor to our warped sense of values. An interesting comment on our values was made by Dick Gregory when he said, "If you kiss a teat, the film is X-rated; if you blow it off, it's general admission."

Between the ages of three and sixteen, the average American child spends more time watching television than he spends in school. In 1964, the average American child between the ages of five and fourteen witnessed the violent destruction of more than 13,000 human beings on television. Although television entertainment does not provide an accurate picture of the real world, many children believe that it does.

A thorough analysis of the television program content of three major North American networks revealed that (a) violence occurred in eight out of ten programs, (b) violence occurred in 93.5 percent of all cartoons directed at children, (c) the "good" guys committed as much violence as the "bad" guys, (d) the pain and suffering accompanying violence is rarely shown, (e) for every bystander who attempted to prevent violence there was another who assisted or encouraged it, (f) nearly half the killers suffered no consequences from their acts, and (g) the majority of Americans interviewed believed that there is too much violence on television.[1]

After a comprehensive analysis of the effects of television violence on children and youth, one study concluded that, "Laboratory studies have shown repeatedly and consistently that observing television violence can make children more willing to hurt others, more aggressive in their play, and more likely to select aggression as a preferred response in conflict situations."[2]

In addition, there is often a significant rise in violent crime rates following some widely publicized tragedy. In some of the most bizarre crimes and violent murders in the United States, the murderers claimed they got the idea from television. An example of negative television modeling was demonstrated in 1966 when NBC-TV aired a film called "The Doomsday Flight" in which a bomb was placed aboard a plane and a ransom was demanded. Thirteen bomb threats were received by various airlines by the end of the week, an

800 percent increase over the previous month. When the film was later shown in Australia the results were similar. Evidence shows, then, that, to a remarkable degree, viewing violence is directly related to aggressive behavior in the young.

The problem with all this violence (in media, in sports, in all areas of life) is that we are providing models which are not worthy of emulation. We see hardened, insensitive heroes who live by violence, suffer very little, represent no high principles, yet are rewarded in the end. This kind of exposure desensitizes children to human suffering and provides them with a multitude of destructive models to emulate.

Perhaps the most obvious message our children see on television is that violence is usually an effective, successful and painless way to achieve a goal. Do we want this norm accepted in our society? If not, then two long-overdue changes are needed: (1) an immediate and sharp decrease in the amount of violence shown, and (2) an equally enthusiastic effort to increase the number of programs designed to teach positive lessons.[3]

What harm is there in taking precautions against increased violence? I cannot think of a single rational objection from among those concerned with human development and quality of life. But some people do object, based upon monetary gains and losses. Although it may be more humanly profitable for society to heed my advice, it may be less profitable from a monetary standpoint for the few who are reaping the financial rewards of violent programing. Ironically it is often these people who direct the course of our nation and our lives.

A report was released by the Surgeon General of the United States on the relationship between television violence and children's aggression. The report was worded so as to lead to misunderstanding. It was so confusing that a New York Times story on the report was headlined, "TV Violence Held Unharmful to Youth." Many of the researchers associated with the report felt that their work had been represented inaccurately, minimizing what seemed to them to be a clear relationship between viewing of TV violence and youngsters' aggressive behavior.

The report was written in a manner that essentially attempted to maintain the status quo. In light of the weight and direction of social science research it is difficult to comprehend this position. However, it becomes more comprehensible when we see how the final committee was selected. The Surgeon General gave the television industry veto power over the selection of individuals who helped write the report. Television executives blackballed some of the most highly respected authorities on the topic, including Leonard Berkowitz and Albert Bandura who have devoted most of their lives to this field. Obviously some of the research conducted by Bandura and Berkowitz, which clearly documents harmful modeling effects of violence, was not what the television executives felt was in their best interest, so they chose to suppress it. In addition, they secured five of the twelve committee positions for their own company executives and company consultants in place of prominent scientists.

Even television executives would have to admit that it is ludicrous to think that private business would continue to pour billions of dollars into television advertising every year if they were not convinced that they could affect values and behavior. Yet these same executives are quick to deny that television programs, which are much more extensive in time and exposure than commercials, have any significant impact on behavior, such as aggression. If products which are often unnecessary or useless can be sold through repeated exposure on television and other media, why not violence?

Unfortunately our "window to the world" has been blurred by commercial interests. Advertising teaches us that we only become valued by others through material gains. It teaches us that all our problems can be solved or relieved by buying some product. Happiness is portrayed as something achieved through a purchase and violence is most often the hook used to get us to hang around for the advertisement. Television rarely seems to focus on products or events that *really* contribute to health and happiness. Much of the creative energy and consultation which goes into programing and advertisements is wasted on material profit when it could easily be directed toward human profit.

If corporation executives, or others, want to bring home film clips, or advertisements to condition themselves to a certain set of dehumanizing values, let them do it in their own homes. But to inflict them on the rest of society is an infringement upon others' rights to grow in a healthy manner. When television enters living rooms throughout the world, it has a serious responsibility to promote positive, humanizing values, rather than negative, dehumanizing values.

When we watch the news, it seems that *everyone* is ruthless, everyone is at war, everyone is bombing and killing, when in fact everyone is not. There's no denying that these ruthless events are occurring, but so are many postive events. You don't hear news about how many countries are at peace, or how many people were not killed (perhaps even saved) or how many good things were done for our fellow man. If, in the news or on film, the proportion of positive and negative events were more in line with the proportion which occurs in society at large, we would take a positive step toward realigning our direction. If today 200 million people engage in predominantly good behaviors and 1 million engage in predominantly bad behaviors, then the proportion of good to bad in the news should be 200 to 1.

Somewhere along the line newspeople got the idea that bad news is good news. The wholesale subscription to this idea results in a serious disservice to society. Extensive research has indicated that bad news negatively affects our willingness to cooperate and to help others. Bad news breaks social bonds and leads to various selfish, distrustful and antisocial behaviors even among "normal" people, while good news does just the opposite. Although these effects are unintended, they are serious and immediate.

What good does it do for us to hear about some bizarre killing day after day? To give such attention to the person who committed this act increases the probability of a similar act occurring in the future. It provides certain viewers with ideas and a way of behaving which was previously not part of their possible repertoire of behavior. In contrast, the more positive (and fewer negative) models that we are confronted with lead to a.greater probability of behaving positively.

For example, it has been found that children who see models who are generous and sharing are more likely to share themselves. Focusing on the good things people do is extremely valuable for a child's development. Why don't we see and hear more about good things?

Maybe it may not sell the news but it certainly sells a more healthy way of life. Then again, it may sell the news if it were attempted.

ARE SPORTS A ROYAL ROAD TO PEACE AND HARMONY?

It has long been maintained that sports, particularly competitive and aggressive sports, serve to reduce aggression by acting as a safety valve to let off steam. This is known as the catharsis theory of aggression. According to this theory participation in, or the viewing of, aggressive acts results in a decrease in aggressive tendencies. The word catharsis implies a purging or cleansing of the emotions that brings about spiritual renewal. Aggressive sports are purported to serve in a cathartic way by dissipating or releasing our aggressive tendencies.

In order to shed some light on this problem as it relates to children's competition, Nelson, Gelfand and Hartmann conducted an experiment in 1969 with five- and six-year-old children. The children were exposed to either an aggressive or nonaggressive adult model and were then engaged in either competitive or noncompetitive games. Following the games each child was observed during free play. The children's play clearly supported the view that competition promotes aggression, even above the heightened aggression normally caused by exposure to an aggressive model. A closer look at the results revealed that children who had experienced failure in the competitive games generally became most aggressive, followed by those who had succeeded. Children who had engaged in non-competitive play were least aggressive in their subsequent free play.

Based upon their extended research, Gelfand and Hartmann in 1975 concluded that rather than reducing "aggressive drive," competitive play produces significant increases in aggression regardless of win-loss outcome. They go on to say that the excitation of competition coupled with the aggressive modeling frequently displayed in children's athletic contests can produce increases in the children's undesirable aggressive responses. There is simply no lessening of aggressive tendencies due to involvement in vigorous competitive physical activity. In actuality, competition heightens, rather than lessens, susceptibility to aggressive influence.

A study was conducted where children played three aggressive games, one called Stomp, one called Scalp, and one called Cover the Spot. In Stomp, each child is given a ping pong ball and the only rule is to smash the other child's ball and protect your own. In Scalp, each child has an arm band on his arm and the only rule is to take the other child's arm band and protect your own. For Cover the Spot, a little spot is put in the middle of the floor and the only rule is that after 20 seconds, the person covering the spot is the winner.

It was found that children who had been trained to play these aggressive games acted more aggressively in situations that weren't related at all. For example, in a playroom, they acted much more aggressively than they had before this kind of training. A followup study using these same games showed that when the aggressive games were followed by an opportunity to electrically shock another person, the children responded more aggressively regardless of whether they won or lost the contest. An earlier study also suggests some lasting or spin off, effects of reinforced aggression in play. Children reinforced for punching a Bobo doll, as compared to children not reinforced, behaved more aggressively in a competitive situation several days later.[4]

Additional light was shed on this question when Larry Leith and I found that nine-year-old organized sport participants scored somewhat higher in general aggressiveness than their nonparticipating peers.

In a followup study, we found a trend toward increased aggression in normal everyday encounters (outside of sport) among ten-year-old boys, based upon the extent of their hockey participation. Nonparticipants in organized sport had the lowest level of general aggressive predispositions, followed by house league players, with the all-star group having the highest level of general predisposition to behave aggressively. These findings are suggestive rather than definitive, and the trend could be interpreted in a variety of ways. For example, the more aggressive children may be the ones going out for sports like hockey, rather than hockey affecting their level of social aggressiveness.

According to Leonard Berkowitz, reinforcing one class of aggressive response can increase the likelihood of another kind of aggressive response as well. For example, people who are reinforced for verbal aggression are subsequently more likely to carry out physical aggression. Berkowitz feels that reinforcing aggression on the football field might well lead to aggressive responses in other settings as well.

When people are highly emotionally aroused, when they "blow their cool," the learned inhibitions and learned discriminations which tell them when and where to behave in a certain way may not work. "Prize fighters and football players know that it's all right to knock their opponent down in the ring or on the football field but not in the street or house. Still, I would bet that if they happen to be angry and not thinking on some occasion, the reinforcements they had previously received for aggression in competition will increase the chance that they will act violently in this other setting as well," points out Berkowitz.

Based on common sense we would expect that after being encouraged and rewarded for hitting numerous times, hitting would take on a different meaning. If hitting is made to seem necessary and desirable, and is reinforced, the social sanctions against hitting would be lightened and the behavior itself would be strengthened. Hitting would no longer be a big deal and dehumanizing another human being in order to hit him would become an accepted norm, particularly if it was thought to help achieve *the goal*.

If combative sports reduce aggressive tendencies off the sport fields, then we would expect to find lots of aggressive sports in peaceful societies and few aggressive sports in warlike societies.

In order to analyze this proposition, R. G. Sipes selected ten warlike and ten peaceful societies and coded them for the presence or absence of combative sports. Of the ten warlike societies, nine had combative sports and only one did not. Of the ten peaceful societies, only two had combative sports. This indicates that combative sports and the tendency to warlike behavior tend to occur together. In addition to having more combative sports, the more warlike societies were found to have higher aggressiveness in that they used more severe punishment. Sipes contends that aggressive behavior may be reduced by eliminating combative or conflict sports rather than by promoting them.

H. Kaufmann said that if the commonly held catharsis position were true, then we should require all children be maximally exposed to violence and bloodshed (through such things as media and games) in order to reduce violent crime and aggression in the streets. However, the available evidence shows that engaging in competitive and aggressive games does not decrease aggressiveness. Physical acts of aggression or violence may reduce immediate tension and exhaust a person for a short period of time, but they also seem to set the stage for more violence in the long run.

If a child is encouraged to be aggressive and is reinforced for his aggressive behavior, there is a greater probability of this behavior occurring in the future. Similarly, if he sees models engaging in and being reinforced for aggressive behavior, he is more likely to engage in aggressive behavior. In addition, modeling influences do not have to be immediate. They may not be expressed in the form of overt behavior until some time in the future.

VIOLENCE AMONG THE FANS

Jose, a high school soccer player, scored three minutes before the final whistle with a beautiful long shot.

As he rushed into the goal after the shot, a fight broke out between the players. Four shots rang out and Jose fell dead with bullet wounds ripping through his mouth, face and arms. He was shot to death by a fan of the opposing team.

In Peru, a referee disallowed a goal in a world class soccer match and the crowd rioted. Before it was over 300 people were killed, 500 were injured, and numerous buildings were destroyed.

In Moscow, a top division soccer player recently assaulted a referee after his club had lost. The assault provoked the following comment from the newspaper Pravda: "This summer we have observed an increasing number of incidents of violation of discipline and sporting ethics on the football field."

Last August, in one of four incidents which disrupted English soccer matches, a spectator was murdered. In another instance, more than 100 people were injured when fighting broke out between rival soccer fans at the West Ham-Manchester United soccer game in England.

In certain areas of the United States, fights and brawls are common events after high school basketball and football games.[5] In some cases these outbreaks have led to death. Some cities have found it necessary to eliminate high school crowds completely in order to curtail the violence.

When winning is vitally important, when scores are easily discernable, when aggression is modeled, when tension is high, when defeat becomes apparent, crowds can "turn ugly." And destructiveness among fans is not only evident when defeat becomes apparent, it also accompanies victory. In 1969 when the Czech hockey team defeated the Russian team in the world championship tournament, highly charged Czechoslovakian youth ransacked the Russian airline office in Prague.

There are so many cases of spectators becoming violent as a result of an emotionally pitched game that we have to wonder why the notion persists that the viewers will lessen their aggressive inclinations by seeing the game. Clearly someone forgot to tell these fans that watching highly competitive or aggressive sports is supposed to subdue their aggressive tendencies.

Larry Leith and I conducted one of the few studies that assessed the effects on the young audience of viewing aggressive and nonaggressive sports. Boys in third, fourth, and fifth grades were divided into three groups. One group was shown a clip from the heavyweight boxing championship between Muhammed Ali and Joe Frazier, which was chosen for its ability to portray three minutes of easily perceived overt aggression. A second group saw a three minute clip from a gymnastics meet which included a floor exercise routine and a still rings routine. This film clip was chosen for its lack of any form of distinguishable overt aggression. A third group served as a control, sitting for three minutes with no film being presented.

The results indicated that the boys who had watched the boxing film showed a significant increase in their inclination to shove or hit a peer if placed in a situation which made them mad. Contrarily, the boys who watched the gymnastics film, as well as those who served as a control, seeing no film, did not show an increased tendency to hit their peers in various hypothetical situations provided in the test.

When asked how the films made them feel, the

majority of the children who saw the boxing film said it made them feel like fighting or hitting someone, while those who saw the gymnastics film said it made them feel happy, good or strong. The findings of this study suggest that the viewing of aggressive sport models serves to increase the overall predisposition toward aggression in the young audience. Several studies have shown similar findings among adult audiences.

Findings of controlled studies support the general proposition that the observation of aggression in sports increases the probability of subsequent aggressive behavior. Aggression modeled by athletes coupled with the increased arousal sometimes surrounding sports competition may help to explain the fights and riots which break out among spectators. The explosion of group violence among fans may also be facilitated by the diffusion of responsibility. No one really feels it is his fault and there is little chance of getting caught.

While aggression may not be a necessary consequence of athletic competition, there is no satisfactory evidence which indicates that athletic competition produces a discharge or relief for pent-up aggression. Sports are no royal road to peace and harmony. . . . not in its violent form. It is interesting to note that in non-violent artistic sports such as skating or gymnastics, I've never heard of a fight in the stands. Have you?

VIOLENCE AMONG THE PLAYERS

It is evident that sports models can have an impact upon viewers' behavior and many of those viewing are children who are themselves players. Youngsters learn many things from their sports heroes. They may learn a new passing combination, to raise their arms after a score, to fling their gloves to the ice before fighting, that winning is all important, or that fighting is an admirable behavior. It depends on what is being modelled and what is being reinforced. It is also largely dependent upon what is highlighted by media coverage.

Sportscasters can promote positive values of sport. However, most "scorecasters" intensify the importance of winning and "crunchcasters" highlight and rerun infractions, penalties, and fights and gasp admirably at the most crushing blows. Perhaps this is part of a conspiracy to "sell" the game.

Most professional hockey players agree that the advertising and selling of the game overemphasizes the fighting and brawling at the expense of educating the crowds about skill and finesse. The advertisements for the NBC game of the week showed a film clip of a hockey fight. In every segment of the heralded "Peter Puck" cartoon series, designed to educate the American fan as to the intricacies of the game, players were characterized as Neanderthal brutes demonstrating every conceivable type of foul with great gusto and relish.[6]

But let's look at some of the negative behavior being modelled in the game itself. In a preseason hockey game between Philadelphia and Montreal, the models had a bench clearing brawl, 332 minutes in penalties, and 15 game misconducts. The game had to be stopped by the referee before the completion of the third period.

That same evening 216 minutes in penalties were called in a "game" between Chicago and Boston. The ice was cleared by the referee late in the second period after a brawl which stopped the game for twenty minutes. Thirty-one players left the benches to join the fight. In the words of Dave Schultz, a sports hero who made his reputation by fighting, "I'm not gonna stop fighting even if I could. It's one of my assets and if it helps win games I'm going to keep fighting."

Apart from the negative values being perpetrated by such aggressive acts, they take their toll on youngsters' physical well being. In 1974, 237 Canadian hockey players suffered eye injuries, including 35 of whom were legally blinded in one eye. In American football, helmets have become offensive weapons and as a result, one third of those U.S. college freshmen recruits tested were found to have cervical spine injury.

These problems are not restricted to what is commonly thought of as contact sports. Bench clearing brawls have now hit major league baseball. Even intramurals which were conceived to provide an alternative to the highly competitive interscholastic program are in some ways worse than what they were designed to replace. There are often more fights in intramural hockey games than in varsity games. Athletes in my classes have participated in girls' intramural and intercollegiate basketball games marred by glaring and shoving matches. A high school basketball coach was visibly upset as she told me that one of her players had kneed the referee in the groin. Even the game of broomball (played with brooms on ice with no skates) which was surely conceived in the spirit of frivolity has been victimized. A full scale fight recently broke out during a university intramural coed broomball game. The benches cleared and about 30 people were on the ice swinging it out with brooms all over the place.

In many competitive sports, players can be both participants in and spectators to aggressive acts. Observing aggressive acts while on the bench or on the side of the field may in itself serve to increase subsequent aggression, particularly if players are in an aroused, competitive state. Thus there is a snowball effect.

To reduce the destructive aggression problem in children's sports, we can begin to teach children proper values and self control the first time they step on the ice or field. We can come up with strategies which make the numerical outcome of the games less crucial and urgent. We can also introduce no-hitting, no-contact versions of "contact" sport. This is working very well in certain football, lacrosse and hockey leagues. However, looking at the system as it exists in a sport like hockey, we must recognize that self control is not generally built in and current rules do not stop aggression. Players know that if they take someone into the penalty box with them, it's not really a penalty because they do not put their team at a disadvantage, and if they go to the penalty box alone they do not really hurt their team unless the other team scores.

One way of discouraging destructive aggression under the present system would be to make the effect of the penalty a certainty rather than a probability, or chance occurrence. Perhaps this could be done by awarding a point to the offended team when a player on the offending team instigates a destructive act. Immediately after the infraction, the scoreboard would change and the offending player would go directly back to his bench, not to a penalty box.

This would provide a great deal more peer pressure and a great deal more reason *not* to act destructively. The same point penalty system could be considered for a collection of three or four minor penalties by one team in a variety of sports.

Another idea is to reward someone who clearly avoids a fight by giving his team an extra player rather than placing so much attention on the inappropriate behavior of the offender.

These suggestions may or may not serve as a stop gap measure. In the final analysis, the only logical way to control destructive aggression is to change the values and self control that players themselves take into the game, or to change the game itself.

Granted, aggression may have entertainment value for some spectators and self esteem value for some players. It may even provide a place of belonging and acceptance for certain people, some of whom may not do much else very well. However, if we wish to have a gentler, more peaceful society then we would be wise to downplay all forms of aggression, even if it happens to be in a film or in a game.

We cannot expect to be entertained by violence and not entertain violence in the streets. We cannot both glorify human destructiveness and expect constructive behavior. If we allow the promotion of rivalry and aggression to inundate children's play and games, we must be prepared to suffer the logical consequences in day-to-day living. This is not to say that sports like hockey and football cannot exist, but rather, if we expect to develop empathy, mutual cooperation, and harmony, they cannot exist in a destructive form.

[1] For more information on these studies, see Ryan, Walters and Brown, and Leith, all listed in the bibliography.

[2,3] The Early Window: Effects of Television on Children and Youth, by R.M. Liebert, J.M. Neale, and E.S. Davidson. See bibliography.

[4] R.N. Johnson in Aggression in Man and Animals, and T.K. Baker and S.J. Ball in Mass Media and Violence. See bibliography.

[5] Throughout this book football refers to American or Canadian style football; soccer refers to European football.

[6] W.R. McMurty, "Investigation into Violence in Amateur Hockey." See bilbilgraphy.

What Do You Mean Aggression, Competition, Dehumanization?

To determine the desirability of a particular behavior, we must examine its means and its ends. The ends, the importance attached to the ends, and the extremes to which one will go to achieve these ends will effect the overall value of a competitive or cooperative event.

The most desirable situations are those where both the means and ends are humanizing. The worst situations are those which have means and ends which are both dehumanizing.

A humanizing relationship reflects the qualities of kindness, consideration, compassion, responsiveness, helpfulness, friendship, and love. A dehumanizing relationship is characterized by a lack of concern for the suffering of another, by cruelty, brutality, and a general disregard for human values.

WHAT'S DEHUMANIZING ABOUT AGGRESSION?

When we think of an aggressive person, we often visualize someone who is outgoing, outspoken, and doesn't take no for an answer. In sports we may think of an individual who never gives up, who is always "hustling" on the court, and who shows great individual initiative in order to complete a goal (or compete for a goal). However, in psychological circles this affirmative "hustling" behavior is referred to as assertive behavior rather than aggressive behavior. Assertive behavior would only fall within the realm of aggression if it were motivated by or resulted in the injury or destruction of others. Assertive behavior is motivated by a desire to achieve a goal *without inflicting harm* on others.

Human aggression involves either an intent to hurt or destroy another or the actual hurting or destroying of another, or both. Aggression is classified primarily by the motivation underlying the act, but to be complete might also take into account the outcome of the act.

The most blatant form of aggression is a forceful act with the intent of injury. If a player intentionally swings his stick at his opponent and smashes him in the head, it is a form of aggression involving both destructive intent and injury. If a player intentionally swings his stick at his opponent and just misses his head, it is also a form of aggression, involving a forceful act with an intent to injure, but no injury. If a player swings his stick and by accident another player skates by and is hit on the head, there is no intent to injure but there is an injury resulting. Some would not classify this as an act of aggression as there was no intent to hit the other person and no intent to hurt. However, a forceful act has resulted in an injury and therefore may be perceived as an aggressive act, even though it may have been unintentional. One player was hurt as a result of another player swinging his stick and because of this injurious outcome it could be classified as accidental aggression.

Hitting within the rules of a game, such as heavy body checking, vicious tackling or blocking, spearing with the helmet, forearming, controlled elbowing, and other forms of "legal" hitting which go on in games, may not be as destructive as illegal hitting but they nonetheless are often destructive. It may be legal, but it can still injure or hurt (and in some cases is intended to hurt), just as "legal" aggression in war kills just as surely as does "illegal" aggression.

Nonphysical acts such as a cutting comment, a cold stare, a vicious letter are also forms of aggression if the primary motivation is to hurt, injure or make someone suffer physically or psychologically. Verbal aggression such as spouting profanities; displaced aggression, such as punching a wall or kicking a locker room door; and symbolic aggression, such as giving someone "the finger," are all forms of aggression which can exist in the sports environment. However, the focus of this discussion is aggression expressed in the form of intentional physical contact between people.

Within this focus, destructive aggression is behavior aimed primarily at hurting another person physically and violence is behavior aimed at destroying another person. As outlined on my physical aggression continuum, (Table I, page 126-7) violence is the most extreme form of aggression involving the exertion of extreme force to destroy, injure or abuse. Destructive aggression normally occurs in sports when someone intentionally sets out to hurt another player in a premeditated manner, or when someone "blows his cool" and "spontaneously" attempts to physically conquer his opponent.

Expressive aggression is a conditioned desire to hit because of the rewards which have been associated with hitting. A good feeling flows from making a good hit but there is no specific intent to injure. A forceful hit becomes synonymous with a job well done and brings praise from others. The aggressive act is therefore an end in itself as well as a means to an end. Expressive aggression sometimes occurs in hitting sports such as football and hockey where players may like to hit but not necessarily to hurt or maim.

With instrumental aggression, the aggressive act is merely instrumental to achieving some other end. There is no intent to hurt or to destroy another person, nor is there pleasure associated with the forceful act itself. The intent is to accomplish a goal which happens to necessitate engaging in an aggressive act. An animal may kill simply in order to eat, but not to hurt, and not for the pleasure of killing. A football player may smash through an opponent simply to make room for his teammate to run through an opening, in order to score. He may have no intention of hurting and may not feel any pleasure in the smashing act itself. It is merely what he has to do to get a job done. It is a means to another end.

Our reaction to an aggressive act will differ depending upon how we perceive the act. Do we feel it was designed to hurt? Do we think it was intentional or unintentional? If someone smashes you to the floor in a game, quickly stops, helps you up, and says "Geez, I'm sorry, I didn't see you there," you will react differently than if someone commits the same act but mutters, "That will teach you, you bastard." Our reactions are largely dependent upon our perception of the intent of the act.

It should be noted that while some forms of aggression are worse than others, all forms of intentional aggression have some dehumanizing component and therefore should not be promoted when alternatives are available.

Did you ask why?

As Dave Meggyesy recounts in his book, *Out of Their League:*

> I know he didn't see me and I decided to take him low. I gathered all my force and hit him. As I did I heard his knee explode in my ear, a jagged, tearing sound of muscles and ligaments separating. The next thing I knew, time was called and he was writhing in pain on the field. They carried him off on a stretcher and I felt sorry—but at the same time, I knew it was a tremendous block and that was what I got paid for. During the rest of my years in the pros, this image would occasionally surface in my mind. This sort of thing happened all the time; it was part of a typical Sunday afternoon in bigtime football. But the conditions that made me feel a confused joy at breaking up another man's body gradually became just one of the reasons why I decided to quit the game. . . . After playing football most of my life, I've come to see that football is one of the most dehumanizing experiences a person can face.

The joy which accompanies the annihilation of another human being is the result of being socialized into a hitting ethic. It is conditioned by the rewards associated with hitting and the negative sanctions against not hitting.

In bigtime college football, to have the reputation of not liking to hit is a serious stigma to carry. Any confusion mixed with the joy of "breaking up another man's body" is a result of also having been exposed to a human ethic.

When George Sauer announced his retirement from the National Football League, he said, "We shouldn't be out there trying to destroy each other, but some people try and make it that way. They have an idea that in order to be really aggressive and obtain the height of football excellence, you have to despise your opponent. I think when you get around to teaching ideas of hatred just to win a ball game, then you're really alienating people from each other and from themselves and are making them strive for false values."

Yet listen to Toronto Maple Leaf president Harold Ballard: "I like a defenseman who will be real tough and nasty. I'm looking for a guy who you can toss raw meat to and he will go wild."

To encourage people to inflict acts of aggression in sports or other areas of life would appear to be of negative social value. Not only are the acts destructive in themselves, but they are also accompanied by dehumanization. Dehumanization is common in many situations of conflict and is particularly evident in physical confrontations ranging from collision sports such as football to war. It may involve attributing negative values to the victim or merely treating him like an object or a machine. Dehumanization makes the destruction of another individual easier, as it is difficult to purposely inflict harm or pain on other human beings unless you can find some way of dehumanizing them.

In situations of conflict, "leaders" therefore often help the destructiveness along by fostering the dehumanization of "the enemy." Once people engage in degrading acts, they then try to convince themselves that the person deserves it, is subhuman anyway, or that he will get them if they don't get him. In this way they justify their destructiveness and provide some excuse for their cruelty. This in turn increases the probability of engaging in similarly destructive acts in the future.

From a human development perspective it would be much more valuable to concentrate on building empathy among people since that would make it more difficult to act aggressively. It has been demonstrated that the more empathy a person has for others, the less likely he is to resort to aggressive or destructive tactics. And it has been demonstrated that a negative relationship exists between empathy and aggressiveness in children.

D. W. Johnson also found a strong relationship between cooperating and taking the emotional perspective of other individuals, i.e., to empathize with others. When fourth grade children who had a greater disposition to compete were compared with those inclined to cooperate, it was found that the more cooperative children were better able to identify how others were feeling and to explain why they were feeling that way.

Cooperation intensifies an individual's concern for others and encourages people to empathize with others. On the other hand, aggression, competition and rivalry intensify conflict and reduce one's concern for the feelings of others, particularly opponents. Therefore competition, at least as it exists in North America, often seems to set the stage for dehumanization and aggression while cooperation sets the stage for humanization and positive alternatives to aggression.

BUT WHAT IS COMPETITION?

Margaret Mead defined competition as the act of seeking to gain what another is endeavoring to gain at the same time. She defined individualistic behavior as an act in which the individual strives toward his goal, without reference to others, and cooperation as the act of working together toward one end. In a situation involving pure cooperative interdependence, a person can attain his goal, if, and only if, others with whom he is linked can attain their goals. In a situation of pure competition an individual can attain his goals, if, and only if, others with whom he is linked cannot attain their goals. Pure competition is oriented toward a single goal, and other competitors for that goal are secondary. The object or goal for which they are competing is of primary importance. They strive to outdo or beat their opponent in order to prove their superiority.

Rivalry is behavior directed against another person, while the object or position for which they compete is secondary. If the major goal is to conquer others or to make sure that they do not achieve their goal, this is rivalry. Ensuring that the opponent is not rewarded is more important than self improvement or being better than others. This can be observed when one person is willing to let his own performance suffer in order to reduce the rewards of a peer. He does not care how well he does as long as he can ensure his peer does poorly.

Another form of rivalry mentioned in a previously discussed study was when one child prevented another child from playing with a toy, even when he knew that he could not play with it himself. He delighted in making sure the other child did not get it. Both sadistic rivalry and destructive aggression are extensions of competition, though competition certainly does not have to be extended to this extreme.

In a competitive situation, reinforcements such as points, a win, positive social feedback, etc., are usually distributed to individuals unequally, based upon their competitive performance. In a competitive game, one's demonstrated ability in achieving the goal or preventing others from achieving the goal is rewarded. This is not to say that in all forms of competition an individual who does not receive the stated game reinforcements is necessarily barred from all reinforcement. A "loser" on the scoreboard may have "won" in terms of having met a personal performance goal, the excitement experienced, a good workout, sheer enjoyment, or positive social feedback from an important person.

So competitive situations do not necessarily have to be purely competitive, either/or situations, although they generally are because so much emphasis has been placed upon the most striking and easily recognizable outcome— the score. The individual's perception of the competitive situation greatly influences his orientation and personal outcome. In cooperative competition the orientation taken into the game is less serious and the scoreboard outcome less vital than in competitive, or pure, competition. The outcome of the game never becomes more important than players' welfare. Competition with others is a means to mutual enjoyment and may also be aimed at improving physical, emotional or social outcomes.

Noncompetitive cooperation moves beyond competition in that the goal is shared and the relationship to the goal holds the cooperating individuals together. Social and other kinds of reinforcement are distributed to individuals equally, based upon their cooperative behavior. In a cooperative game, one's demonstrated contribution to a collective goal is rewarded and the game reinforcements are shared by all participants.

With cooperative helpfulness the goal is shared only through the relationship of the helper to the individual whose goal it actually is. The emphasis is on helping another person and not upon the goal itself. There is pleasure in the act of helping and in seeing others achieve their goal. Cooperative helpfulness and love are extensions of cooperation.

A few examples will help clarify these categories. In the morning I usually run down a little country road, alongside a lake, with a friend. If my primary goal were to maintain or improve my own health, this would be individualistic behavior. If my goal were to prove my superiority by running faster than she did with absolutely no regard for her welfare, this would be competitive competition. If my goal were to prevent her from achieving a goal she wanted to achieve this would be rivalrous behavior. And if my primary goal were to help her achieve her goal then this would be cooperative helpfulness.

In the above situation I am personally operating on two levels, individualistic and helpful. I am interested in improving my own health and I am also interested in helping my friend achieve her goals. There is no conflict here, as would be the case between rivalry and helpfulness which denotes conflicting motivations. On the contrary, I cannot try to both put her down and help her up at the same instant.

Let's use as another example an activity which some people may be able to relate to better, sexual intercourse. Some sort of cooperation between two individuals is normally required to engage in this act. However, if the primary goal is to reach a climax without reference to what the other person is experiencing, then this is an individually oriented behavior. If the goal is to work (or play) together to share the enjoyment of the process (the means) as well as the climax (the end), without comparative reference to others, this is noncompetitively cooperative. If satisfaction becomes fused with the satisfaction of the partner, this relationship becomes a totally humanizing example of cooperative helpfulness.

It should be pointed out that cooperation is not always humanizing nor is competition always dehumanizing. For example, cooperation focused on the destruction of others cannot be considered desirable nor can competition resulting in the betterment of all parties be considered undesirable. Similarly cooperation and competition are not necessarily polar opposites which occur independently of one another. There are degrees of competition and cooperation, and sometimes interactions between the two. For example, members of the same team can cooperate to achieve a common goal like winning the game, but can compete to make the starting lineup, or to be the highest scorer. Members of one team may cooperate in order to be better competitors or may compete to be the best cooperator. A case could be made for having two separate continuums, one extending from competition to non-competition and the other extending from cooperation to noncooperation.

When analyzing primitive cultures, Mead found it necessary to distinguish between collective activity and individual activity. Collective activity and individual activity refer to observable behavior but not to one's intent or goal. Cooperative, competitive and individualistic behavior were defined in terms of the major motivation of the participant. "So a man who hunts alone in the bush in order to contribute his kill to the communal feast is engaged in an individual activity in as much as he is working alone, but he is nevertheless engaged in a cooperative enterprise," she points out in writing about the Arapesh of New Guinea.

Consequently collective activities are not necessarily cooperative and individual activities are not necessarily individualistic or competitive. The reason for engaging in an activity gives a clue as to the nature of the activity. We must consider the structure, the intent of the act as well as the overt behavior. The perception one takes into the specific structure or activity largely determines the nature of the activity. In cooperative competition, other people, including competitors, are always more important than the goal for which they compete. The structure may be competitive, but the people playing within the structure are cooperative. Perhaps this is what allows people in certain cultures to participate with others in a competitive game, yet behave in a friendly, cooperative and helpful way. The same "competitive" game, with the same stated rules, can be played very differently in other cultures, and by diversified groups within the same culture. If competition is to exist, we can humanize competition, so that it becomes more cooperative.

As a society and as individuals we have the capacity to fall anywhere along the competition-cooperation continuum. People and nations engage in behaviors which they feel the situation calls for and exhibit those behaviors socially sanctioned by their society. If our lives were oriented predominantly towards the humanizing end of the scale, occasional diversions in the other direction would not pose the serious problems with which we are now faced.

For many people in our society, competitive competition has become the customary mode of response to almost all situations. For others, rivalry or putting people down has become the norm. Some people delight in others' despair. But cooperation can also become a normal way of responding to the environment. The reason I feel it is important to make helping a habit is because I believe that by promoting mutually beneficial helping habits we can begin to solve many of society's most dehumanizing problems.

Contrary to what is commonly thought, serving self (egotism) and serving others (altruism) are not contradictory or mutually exclusive. As Selye writes, in Stress Without Distress:

> The instinct for self preservation need not conflict with the wish to help others. Altruism can be regarded as a modified form of egotism, a kind of collective selfishness that helps the community in that it engenders gratitude. By making a person wish that we should prosper because of what we have done—and, hence, are likely to do for him again—we elicit goodwill. This is perhaps the most humane way of assuring our security (homeostasis) in society. . . . By creating gratitude and trust we induce others to share our natural wish for our own well being.

One often best serves himself by helping others. At first glance this may not seem to be the case because the immediate payoff might not appear to be there, but a more thorough analysis certainly leads one to this conclusion.

Individuals will want to cooperate once they realize

that it is in their own best interest to do so. Cooperative habits will develop when people recognize that cooperating, helping and sharing can be very reinforcing for oneself as well as for others. We come to place greater value on others (and upon helping others) once we recognize that this helping relationship makes us feel more fulfilled and makes others respond to us more positively. The more situations allow us to experience reinforcing cooperative relationships, the more predominant these responses will become within our own lives and within our society.

The most basic conclusion that came out of Margaret Mead's work with primitive peoples was that competitive and cooperative behavior on the part of individual members of a society is fundamentally conditioned by the emphasis of various structures within that society. The goals for which individuals will work, as well as the means by which they pursue them, are culturally determined.

Once there is development of mutually positive interest in one another's welfare, each person receives vicarious pleasure from the other person's pleasure. Under such circumstances, even if the original goals around which cooperation developed are attained, or changed, a continuing basis for cooperative relations is created.[1] In essence the development of an interest in the welfare of others provides a source of motivation and commitment to a cooperative ethic, and as such provides the basis for continuing cooperation.

---

[1]*See Deutsch (1962) in bibliography.*

A Capacity To Enhance: A Capacity To Destroy

My own life has revolved around games and sports. To make them what they are capable of being is my objective. I would like nothing better than to proclaim that sports are all the wonderful things that they have been cracked up to be: character builders, aggression reducers, builders of moral values, and so on. But it doesn't happen to be true. If, in the course of my lifetime, I could say in all honesty that games and sports have become psychologically and morally beneficial to the vast majority of children, we will have accomplished something significant, indeed. Unfortunately we are not yet at that point.

FIRST PEACE

"I hope they realize that the Olympics are dead"

anais nin, her clear eyes into mine,
and so finally after years of silence
I begin to speak out

so much crowding into my head to say, to vomit up
to scream, to cry quietly
and finally to accept and breathe deep
and feel the weight of it gone
and free at last

I have been insane the past years of my life
and am just now coming into my own self,
my own voice

I was the all American girl, the winner, the champion,
the swell kid, good gal, national swimmer,
model of the prize daughter bringing it home for dad
I even got the father's trophy

I was also jock, dyke, stupid dumb blond
frigid castrating domineering bitch,
called all these names in silence,
the double standard wearing me down
inside

on the victory stand winning my medals
for father and coach
and perhaps a me deep down somewhere
who couldn't fail because of all the hours
and training and tears
wrapped into an identity of muscle and power
and physical strength
a champion,

not softness and grace

now, at 31, still suffering from the overheard
locker room talk, from the bragging and swaggering
the stares past my tank suit
insults about my muscles
the fears, the nameless fears
about my undiscovered womanhood
disturbing unknown femininity,
femaleness

feminine power

I learned of a teammate's suicide
the dam has broken
her death has plunged me deep out of myself
to the other side

I've got sisters out there and they need my voice
just as I've needed theirs all these years.

the Olympics is dead; long live sports

the love of sports lives
the love of the female athlete for her sport lives

the old reasons for competing are dead
the petty jealousies, the psychological games,
the fear trips, the winning winning winning

one four SEVEN anyone for EIGHT
gold medals dangling from my neck?

when I swam competitively in the state of Florida
as a teenager
my coach used to enter me in every event possible

"good experience" he would say

I remember feeling embarrassed at 14 walking up to the
starting block in the 13 and 14 year old age group,
the 15 and 16 year old age group,
the senior women's age group
in the same meet,
and sweeping over everyone

WINNING WINNING WINNING

proving over and over again
how great I was

as I look back on it now I understand

I was put into events by my coach who was excited
about having a young state breaststroke champion
as his swimmer

he was just coming into his own as a coach
and was building a powerful club
he was fighting the fight all dedicated coaches fight
to get his sport and his swimmers recognized

but as a swimmer I was his tool
as a young girl athlete under his dominating personality
I had nothing to say about what I would swim

so I kept bringing in the medals
until it wasn't how well I could do against the best
in my best events
but how many team points I could amass during a meet
to help the cause of swimming as a sport

him as a winning coach
and of course me as a state champion

I loved swimming until it became a nightmare for me
until it turned into a fear trip
when I became a winner afraid to lose
because America can't love a loser,
a second place person

I loved the thrill of international competition
until nationalism and commercialism
and finally murder itself
causes me to reevaluate why

why I ever wanted to win
in the first place

just what are we winning
if the costs are so high
a loss of identity,
a loss of self
a loss of soul
a sacrifice to the god gold
gold gold and more gold

my God, where have our values gone
that a fellow athlete swimmer
after brilliantly coming back from his defeat in '68
to victory in '72
has to cash in for the pictures
drink milk signs make me puke

sports is dying
how you play the game means nothing
it's winning and how many and how much
it's me me me me me
as it has to be if you want to win
but at what price winning?

every waking hour in the pool to get better to win more
to dedicate yourself so much to one thing
that you block out the rest of life

when to take time to take a walk
a park
the sea
a kiss

to fight to free the athletes from their ridiculous rules

is it all medals and money America?

American sports scene filled with racism and sexism
corrupt and greedy lying lustful people
who are doing it in the name of the athlete
in the name of the country
in the name of the all American way
gone mad

it's time to get it all out and look at it
a good long hard look
at what we have become in American sports
now another battleground for pent up hate
and frustrations
where backroom decisions and confused officials
bloody the sports world just as
surely as the gun

the athlete is the political hostage here, now

he works hard to win
the coach is dedicated and tries to help him
both have desire to please each other

all athletes strive for the best they can put out
why then should SEVEN be more important than one
gold medal
in the long run
who cares how many

no more heroes please
no more gods to live up to and worship

can't we do it for the fun of it,
for the love of it,
instead of the gold of it

can't we get off the tit of the sacred cow,
the false idol
and into what it's really all about,
love
doing it
for the love of it

Barbara Lamblin, 1975
My Skin Barely Covers Me

ENCHANTMENT OR DISENCHANTMENT

The games people play have become more important than the people themselves. At this point, competition begins to have a destructive impact and games become self effacing rather than self enhancing. In sports, as in other areas of life, if victory is made to seem important enough, people will do literally anything in their frantic clutches at it. The production syndrome is clearly overemphasized when people become inwardly or outwardly destructive in pursuit of victory or in fear of defeat.

As pointed out by Bertrand Russell in the 1930's, the lives of many individuals seem to have been permeated by the psychology of a 100 yard dash. They concentrate too much on winning and remain too highly distressed to be happy. "It is not only work that is poisoned by the philosophy of competition; leisure is poisoned just as much," said Russell in 1930.

What Russell pointed out years ago is even more true today. In many cases it is impossible to distinguish between work and leisure. When all of life becomes a race, the greatest pleasures and highest values are abandoned. It is ironic that we have become slaves to the competitive ethic, to the materialistic ethic, which in theory were to free us to enjoy a heightened quality of life.

The only justification for sports is to enrich the quality of our lives. The more lives that can be enriched through involvement in sports, the more valuable they become. However, it has become obvious that sports are not necessarily good for people, as was once supposed, nor, I might add, are they inherently bad. Rather, they have the capacity to be either beneficial or harmful depending upon the kinds of experiences they provide.

For every positive psychological or social outcome in sports, there are possible negative outcomes. For example, sports can offer group membership or group exclusion, acceptance or rejection, positive feedback or negative feedback, a sense of accomplishment or a sense of failure, evidence of self worth or evidence of worthlessness.

Sports can develop cooperation and a concern for others, but they can also develop intense rivalry and a complete lack of concern for others. Activities can be structured to reduce tension but they can also lead to unhealthy levels of distress, particularly when winning is overemphasized. In essence, the sports environment has the capacity to enhance as well as the capacity to destroy.

The Associated Press carried a story about a 12-year-old boy in Cincinnati who was ordered to go to a Little League baseball practice against his will, and was later found hanged in a wooded area near his home. A baseball glove lay nearby. The distraught coach who implied that the boy didn't really like sports, "at least not baseball," asked the question which we should all be asking ourselves today: "I wonder if I pushed him too hard?"

An isolated incident? Perhaps. However, suicide itself is no longer a rare phenomenon. Well over 25,000 Americans kill themselves every year. In the past few years the number of youngsters who have killed themselves has tripled and suicide ranks as the second largest killer of youth in Canada.

Why do young people kill themselves? Can they be prevented from doing so? The best suicide prevention is a meaningful relationship with other persons who say, by their actions, "I care, you matter to me."

In a unique study on psychological health, Abraham Maslow reported that extremely psychologically healthy people feel accepted, unanxious, safe, loved, and loving. They have a strong sense of self respect, feelings of belonging, and seem to be developing to the full stature of which they are capable. In addition, extremely well adjusted people have a deep feeling of identification, sympathy, and affection for fellow human beings. They have a genuine desire to help the human race. It was as if they view everyone as members of the same family.

Maslow outlined the following characteristics as being most representative of extremely psychologically healthy persons:

Acceptance of self, others and nature
Spontaneity, simplicity, naturalness
Creativity
Continued freshness and appreciation of basic goods of life
Problem centered (rather than ego centered)
Deep and profound interpersonal relations
Strong democratic character (as opposed to authoritarian)

Autonomy, independence, self-determination, responsibility

Unhostile sense of humor

Efficient perception of reality and comfortable relations with it

Resistance to enculturation to society as it exists

Strong ethical and moral standards

Capable of having and enjoying peak experiences often

Capable of enjoying solitude and privacy

Deep feelings of identification, sympathy and affection for others

Experiences in human cooperation are the most essential ingredient for the development of psychological health. Cooperative interaction with others is imperative for developing self acceptance, trust, self confidence, and personal identity, which are foundations for a person's psychological well being. Consequently there are no skills more important to a human being than the skills of cooperative social interaction.

As I reflect upon the qualities and experiences which are so closely linked to psychological health I ask, "Are these the kinds of qualities and experiences that are manifested in most sports environments?"

For example, in little league, do most youngsters feel that they are accepted and that others care about them regardless of their athletic prowess? Do they feel they are part of a meaningful and secure link in a truly cooperative venture? I wonder if the young baseball player who snuffed out his own life felt this kind of caring and acceptance in his little league setting.

Both children and adults need to feel accepted and to feel they have a meaningful role to play in order to experience life to its fullest and to feel satisfied with their existence. Acceptance is reflected by such things as expression of affection, demonstration of concern about problems faced by others, availability to provide help when needed, friendly shared activities, and general harmony within a relationship or group. Acceptance is expressed by showing an overall warmth to a child or peer, by pointing out contributions in an especially warm way, by taking the time to be with, share with, and help someone, by giving people time to participate fully and by showing a genuine interest in what they do and say. In short, acceptance is demonstrated by treating a person as if he or she is a worthy individual.

During the developing years when the somewhat fragile self concept is still being formed and tested, much of a child's world revolves around active play and games. Without minimal levels of acceptance and appropriate models in these environments, a child appears to be at a real disadvantage in terms of developing positive self perceptions and appropriate modes of social behavior.

What kinds of people are children exposed to in activity environments? What kinds of experiences do they have? What kinds of behaviors are reinforced? Are children rewarded for honesty, for sharing, for respecting the rights and feelings of others, or are they rewarded for disregarding the rights and feelings of others, for dishonesty, and for destructive aggression? Are players encouraged to be self reliant by such things as self organization and self officiating or is dependency nurtured when officials and coaches "call all the shots"? Are participants given the freedom to take a chance, to improvise, to be creative, or is there a preoccupation with outcome, with winning, with authoritarianism?

In an article on Little League football entitled "Taking the Fun Out of a Game," Underwood spoke of six- and seven-year-olds ("little warriors") in full armor playing organized, competitive tackle football; of eight-year-olds having to run wind sprints after practice for "crying out loud;" of coaches and parents calling little children stupid, crybaby, and dumb ass for behaviors which are normal *for children*; of adults falsifying birth certificates and giving young children diet pills to get them into a certain division where they would have the winning edge; of coaches playing only the best even though the others practice five nights a week; of fights among adult spectators from opposing teams; of a coach injecting a stimulant into the oranges to give the team a winning boost; and of coaches mishandling children and bringing eight-year-olds to tears daily. One coach was quoted as screaming, "You're gonna block if I have to kick your ass all afternoon." The eight-year-olds toward whom this abuse was directed reportedly turned to jelly and walked off the field crying.

Underwood added that in order to deal with the problem of some children not being allowed to play in games, one league introduced a rule whereby every child had to play a series every quarter. A recorder was responsible for jotting down the players' numbers *as they went on the field* to ensure that everyone got some playing time. One coach worked out a "winning" scheme to get around this rule. He sent in several players, supposedly to replace several other players, but one of the same players who just went on the field mixed himself up in the huddle and then ran off with the players coming off the field. It took five games before the recorder noticed the same player going on to the field and then coming off, without playing. When the young lad was asked if he had played at all during the year, he said, "No, I just run in and out."

The league called a special meeting to decide what should be done. At this meeting the sponsor for the team in question spoke up, waved his checkbook, and announced that if a decision in any way went against his team, his sponsorship would be withdrawn. The league needed sponsors, so the issue was never allowed to come to a vote. Pee Wee football appears to be an expensive sport, in more ways than one.

Despite the fact that highly competitive sports structures, in the hands of insensitive adults, have the capacity to destroy children, sports also have the potential to enhance many lives by providing funfilled, rewarding activities and opportunities to share and interact with others. For some, sports can also provide a positive medium for self actualization.

Positively oriented sports and physical activities can contribute immensely to one's quality of life. An invigorating game, an exciting or well executed play, a new move, a leisurely sail, a refreshing ski, a scenic jog, a peaceful canoe ride, can be the most enjoyable and rewarding part of the day for many people. Good times with friends and exhilarating personal sensations should be a natural part of sports. It shouldn't be a case where we either play the competitive aggressive game or we're made to feel unacceptable or out of place, so we get out. Instead, if we play a cooperative, friendly game, we should be made to feel totally acceptable. If people begin to have fun, to play constructively, then a welcome place will be made for many more in the world of sports.

When we play broomball down on the lake on Wednesday nights, cooperation among all team members, male and female, young and old, is very evident with everyone being given an opportunity to handle the ball. Setting up less skilled players for a scoring attempt and running good passing plays is as much fun as any other aspect of the game. People on one team sometimes take great delight in seeing someone on the opposing team, who is not noted for scoring, make a goal even though it is against them. Because of the attitude we bring to the game we simply can't lose. I always leave feeling better than when I went. We don't allow the score to get in the way of our enjoyment, of our friendly interaction.

By turning people away from physical activities, usually through exposing them to distressful competition and by making them feel anxious, self conscious, or as if they are not good enough, we are indeed robbing them of a certain heightened quality of life. However, positive social experiences, enjoyable experiences, and self development in sports do not have to be a random occurrence. They can be calculated and international. Activity environments can be constructed to meet the participant's needs, to foster desirable behavior, and to influence the participant's psychological being in a positive direction.

PRODUCTION AND FUN

Surveys have revealed that North Americans view fun as being highly significant in terms of having a

PHYSICAL AGGRESSION CONTINUUM

BEHAVIOR CATEGORY	ORIENTATION	PRIMARY MOTIVATION
Violence	Antihuman	To destroy another through extreme brutality or extreme force. Satisfaction in destroying others.
Destructive Aggression	Antihuman	To hurt, to inflict harm, to injure another. Satisfaction in hurting others.
Expressive Aggression	Self Oriented	To make a good hit, to wipe someone out. Satisfaction in hitting rather than in hurting or destroying. Pleasure associated with hit itself.
Instrumental Aggression	Goal Oriented	To achieve a goal or accomplish a task. Hurtful act is the means to the goal. No intent

		to hurt or destroy and no satisfaction in the aggressive act itself.
Accidental Aggression	Unintentional	Injurious contact occurs by accident with no intent and no satisfaction in the act itself or in the outcome of the act.
Assertive Behavior[1]	Goal Oriented	To achieve a goal or accomplish a task effectively. No aggression and no intent of aggression involved. Individual initiative provides the means to the goal. Not classified in the realm of aggression unless it involves intent to injure, injury, or both.

[1] *Commonly thought of as aggression but not a form of aggression unless it falls under one of the other categories above it.*

satisfying life, feeling good, and learning things more easily. A sense of fun is an important component of our quality of life. In a 30-year followup of people who had been studied as children, those who had the most interesting and fulfilling lives were those who had managed to keep a sense of playfulness at the center of their lives. A link has been established between fun and interaction with others.[1]

In a study I did with Michel Bouet, some interesting themes of fun and anti-fun for young people were revealed. Fun flourished when there was a sense of togetherness, while sharing with others; when there was a sense of freedom from obligation, evaluation and pressure; and when there was a sense of spontaneity, newness and creativity. New things and novel experiences, reversing structures and situations, learning as a creative experience, experiencing things together, and sharing experiences in a pressure free setting were all important components of fun. Fun was killed by the fear of degradation, the fear of rejection, and by these events themselves; by the physical or emotional destruction of others; by a sense of obligation and evaluation; by strictly serious events; and by boring, repetitious, totally predictable, or frustrating events.

For young adults, fun was most prevalent in free flowing activities which were shared with others and where the importance of performance and evaluation was played down. It is interesting to note that as games become increasingly more serious, more performance oriented, more production oriented, there is less and less fun.

H. Hyland found this to be true even for five- and six-year-old children who indicated that the "funnest" things they did were low keyed types of activities without emphasis on regulations or evaluation.

At another level, every professional player interviewed by W.R. McMurtry believed he learned his true skills and love of the game away from competitively structured leagues and adult supervision. This is one of the greatest ironies of all. Adult obsessions with victory may in the long run destroy the most essential ingredient of all in developing children's skill—sheer love of the game.

Time and time again athletes, particularly high calibre athletes, tell me, "I liked it when I started but later it wasn't fun anymore." Perhaps this is why many top athletes retire from their sport never to play again. I've seen it in hockey, in track, in gymnastics, in swimming, in soccer, in practically every sport. An outstanding professional football player recently told me that the most fun he ever had in football was playing touch at the end of the street. "That's what I really enjoyed," he said. Now all that was gone and "It's simply a business, there's great emphasis on winning, on being mean, on hitting and hurting others, there's negative consideration for others."

When you first put a youngster on a trampoline, he is so excited and has so much fun that there's no time to be concerned with how well he does. It doesn't matter! Perhaps this orientation must change for sports to become a medium of high level achievement. However, for most people, sports can be most vauable by providing something other than another medium in which to be judged a success or a failure.

In North America it is not uncommon to lose from 80 to 90 percent of our registered organized sports participants by 15 years of age. There appears to be an increasing trend for youth to opt out earlier and earlier. In one Ontario community, the recreation director stated, "Our statistics show us we have 1,497 people of secondary school age in our community and yet only 160 are registered to participate in our three major sports associations. I reported a number of months ago that we are placing too much emphasis on the development of skills and competition and not enough on fun and participation. This has not been changed."

Eliminations seem to be a long term, ongoing process. Although it can occur at a very early age, the effects may last a lifetime. A. C. Burgess found that middle aged men who were nonparticipants in physical activity had experienced less favorable childhood sports environments than physically active middle aged men. An earlier study I did with eight- and nine-year-old participants and nonparticipants in organized sport showed that many of the children who had opted out of sports had undergone negative experiences and indicated that they never wanted to be involved in sports again.

In another study I did, all the elementary school age sport dropouts interviewed indicated they dropped out for reasons which can be attributed to an emphasis on destructive competition. Expressed reasons for dropping out can be roughly categorized as follows:

1. Forty percent dropped out because of lack of exposure in the form of playing time—always an extra, hardly ever get in, ride the bench.
2. Sixty percent dropped out because of lack of exposure to successful or rewarding experiences—

no fun, not good enough, strike out, never get the puck.

Both of these categories represent a lack of meaningful involvement for the child. Restricted involvement and the absence of rewards in general tend to lead to feelings of unworthiness, unacceptance and unfun, in that particular environment. In turn this leads to a rejection of sport as a viable alternative.

For many children competitive sports operate as a failure factory which not only effectively eliminates the "bad ones" but also turns off many of the "good ones." The programs, by their present structure and emphasis, and the agents of these programs often appear to work together to eliminate children, particularly if they are of lesser skill levels. For the majority of the children the goals and rewards in terms of positive outcomes are consistently placed out of reach.

Many children and many adults are made to feel that they are not good enough to participate. Perhaps this is an unintentional message but it is nonetheless extremely effective in restricting involvement.

"The winner-loser syndrome has paralyzed the average American into passive spectatordom . . . The stakes are too high for most men to afford. It's safer for men to appoint surrogates to win for them while they watch the contest over a glass of beer," say T. Boslooper and M. Hayes. Yet every child and every adult is good enough to interact, to share, to enjoy, to have some excitement, and to have fun while actively involved in play, games or sports.

Jane McNally conducted a study with over 700 high

school students to assess their reasons for not participating more in sports. She found that for both males and females, the single most important factor restricting participation was "not enough fun." The students indicated that they would play more sports if there were more opportunities to play "just for fun." As it is now they felt that "even when we play for fun, the other kids get uptight about playing well."

When competitive cross country skiing dropouts, from the Canadian arctic, were asked what they thought was most important in sports, not one mentioned winning. The overwhelming majority (90 percent) felt that having fun and playing together—cooperating—were the most important things in sports. These northern skiers totally rejected the commonly stated dictum that you have to be good at something to have fun doing it.

Similarly when 10- to 12-year-old hockey players in Kanata, Ontario, were asked, "Do you have to be good at hockey to have fun?" 90 percent of them said, "no." You may have to be good to be allowed to play but youngsters overwhelmingly agree that you do not have to be good in order to have fun playing.

For youth of all ages, having fun is undoubtedly a priority in games and sports as became evident in a recent study wherein every single young hockey player questioned felt that having fun in hockey was important, with 80 percent indicating that it was *really* important. When asked what makes hockey fun, 30 percent of the players said, playing with others (e.g., playing together, playing with friends, teamwork) and 37 percent said just playing the game and being a part of the action. Another 11 percent said hockey was fun when they played with good sports.

In response to a question about what makes hockey not fun, slightly over half of the players referred to aggression or violence, such as fighting, spearing, dirty play, getting flattened, etc. The remainder of the players referred to outgrowths of placing too much emphasis on winning (e.g., restricted participation, pressure) along with the distress associated with losing. Seventy percent of the players indicated they would like to play hockey when they didn't have to worry about who won. Only 4 percent felt that winning was the most important thing in hockey but 75 percent personally thought that other people (peers, coaches or parents) felt winning was most important.

Children tend to act in ways that fulfill the expectations of others, particularly if the others are important to them. Consequently, their behavior on the ice or on the field is probably more reflective of how they feel important people think they should behave than what they themselves think. They learn what is acceptable and correct by interacting with significant people. They are *taught* that winning is what counts, since they certainly do not begin feeling this way. Initially the child plays for fun, for the sheer enjoyment of the game, for stimulation and positive interaction with others. Winning is unimportant, irrelevant; fun is extremely important.

For fun to flourish, the imprisoning chains of the fear of failure must be removed. Feelings of acceptance appear to be a necessary condition for fun and are often felt along with it. Cooperation, mutual assistance, and positive interaction seem to offer the best occasions for fun. Sharing experiences amplify the fun. In games and sport, if we can focus on self acceptance, cooperation and fun, we will contribute something of great value to the quality of our children's lives.

This is precisely what most parents say they want for their children. When mothers and fathers of a group of six- to eight-year-old hockey players were asked what they would like their children to get out of the sports experience, the vast majority (80 percent) mentioned learning to work together and to get along with others as the priority item. In addition, 93 percent of the parents felt that having fun was extremely important or very important. Yet a small minority of people, some of whom are outspoken and powerful, direct sports away from the beneficial experience that most people would like it to be. It's time the majority begin to redirect that course.

To provide a new direction for positive self development through sport means that important people, young and old, have to respond to participants in a positive and accepting manner. It means that expectations and goals have to be readjusted and that priorities have to change. It also means that new orientations and new kinds of games have to be introduced. Games of acceptance must replace games of rejection. If we can let each child feel acceptable and give each child a meaningful role to play within the activity environment, we will be well on our way toward solving most of the major psycho-social problems which presently permeate games and sports. This is one reason why it is so important to create games and learning environments where no one *feels* like a loser.

[1]*For more information see Bruner (1975) and Goffman (1961) in the bibliography.*

Cooperative Game Structures

Games represent a key joint in any society. To turn this society toward peaceful, humane change, we can begin with reform in games. Some intellectuals have ignored this aspect of our lives believing somehow that games are beyond serious consideration. They are mistaken. "There is nothing trivial about the flight of a ball, for it traces for us the course of the planet. . . . How we play the game may turn out to be more important than we imagine, for it signifies nothing less than our way of being in the world."[1]

THE POTENTIAL OF COOPERATIVE GAMES

Games are an extremely powerful means of shaping behavior. Consider a game like poker. Let's suppose you wanted to be totally honest, open and generous while playing. What do you think would happen? It was tried once as an experiment. The experimenter revealed his hand honestly and offered to share his winnings out of generosity. First the others laughed. When he persisted, they got mad and wouldn't let him play anymore. The fact is, you cannot be open, honest and generous and play a serious game of poker at the same time.

Society can be likened to a series of very complicated poker games. Each situation has rules, rewards and punishments which when combined make players act in a

COMPETITION—COOPERATION CONTINUUM

BEHAVIOR CATEGORY	ORIENTATION	PRIMARY MOTIVATION
Competitive Rivalry	Antihuman	To conquer another. To prevent others from achieving their goal. Satisfaction in putting others down and ensuring others do not achieve their goals.
Competitive Competition	Goal Oriented (against others)	Competition against others is a means to achieving a single mutually desired goal such as being faster or better than others. The goal is of primary importance, the welfare of the other competitors is secondary. Competition is sometimes aimed at the devaluation of others.
Individualism	Self Oriented	To pursue an individual goal. To do well. To do one's best. Focus is on personal accomplishments, self development or self improve-

		ment without competitive or cooperative reference to others.
Cooperative Competition	Goal Oriented (considering others)	A means to achieving a personal goal which is not mutually exclusive nor an attempt to devalue or destroy others. The welfare of competitors is always more important than the extrinsic goal for which they compete.
Noncompetitive Cooperation	Goal Oriented (with others)	To achieve a goal which necessitates working together and sharing. Cooperation with others is a means to achieving a mutually desired goal and the goal is also shared.
Cooperative Helpfulness	Humanistic-Altruistic	To help others achieve their goal. Cooperation and helping is an end in itself, rather than a means to an end. Satisfaction in helping others achieve their goals.

certain way, not for an hour or two as in a poker game, but for most of their lives. Just as a game like poker makes players behave in a closed and greedy manner so the rules of the games of life make people behave in certain ways for all their lives.[2]

The game of soldier can turn us into killers, once we decide to play. In times of conflict, a good, pure All American lad may take part in a mass murder. This action grows out of game plans, rules and objectives to which certain leaders commit themselves and to which certain "players" are subjected. While some games required killing, other games may demand and elicit dishonesty on a regular basis. A person may practice it so much in one setting that it is used as a matter of course in other settings as well. However, the same power of games which can prevent people from being honest and loving can be turned around to encourage these behaviors. Different games designed another way can serve a noble purpose another day.

When we play a particular game, we enter a mini-society which can shape us in a variety of directions. Once we have been shaped by the rules, the responses of others, the rewards and punishments, we become part of the game and begin to shape others. In this way the game takes on a life and power independent of the players.

Instead of creating mini-societies or games that reflect in purified form the competitiveness, dishonesty and greed of the larger society, why not develop games that create, in miniature, the utopias in which we would like to live? Why not create and play games that make us more cooperative, honest and considerate of others? Why not use the transforming power of games to help us become the kinds of persons we really would like to be?

Many of our behavioral foundations are thought to lie in children's play and games. R. Havinghurst has pointed out that games are essential in learning human morals. Jean Piaget, as well as many other researchers, has made it very clear that it is primarily through physical activity that a child learns how the world works and how to function within that world. The physical world is a natural one for children's development. Play, organized as games and sports, prepares people for life. In fact, the games that children play become their games of life. If they learn that might makes right, that winning is the only thing, that they must follow the game plan at all costs, then these behaviors may surface through deception, lies, cheating and perhaps violence in the game of life itself. If S.L. Washburn and C.S. Lancaster were correct when they said that the skills for killing and the pleasures of killing were normally developed in play, then certainly the rudiments of cooperative behavior can be developed through children's play. If play patterns prepare children for their adult roles, we had better be sure that the roles they are being prepared to exhibit are desirable ones.

A crucial psychological function of play and games is self validation along with the development of positive interpersonal skills. Cooperative games that we have developed have been designed with this point in mind and many are aimed at preventing social problems from arising *before* they become problems. We focus on setting the conditions for developing a positive sense of self and of others, rather than waiting for problems to surface and then attempting to deal with them. Our concerted effort has been primarily at the preventative level with young children.

Preschoolers spend countless hours playing. When they first enter nursery school or kindergarten, play is often a predominant activity even within the classroom setting. As children grow older, school becomes less play and more work, less active and more passive. However, the child's continuing desire for *active* involvement is obvious when a group of children enters the gym or goes out for recess after being cooped up in a classroom all morning. Much of the child's time outside the classroom revolves around play and games.

This desire for active involvement appears to transcend cultures. W. Zuk who taught in different settlements in the Canadian arctic found that games can make children who are indifferent to schoolwork come to life and participate with interest. I.S. Mitchell reported similar interest in physical pursuits and relative disinterest in formal schooling among Australian Aboriginal children.

In the early years, why not center school around children's natural desire for activity? Why not encourage children to learn through active play and games? Why not allow free and independent play, as well as design cooperative interdependent play? Physically active learning sessions can provide a medium for positive cognitive, motor and social development. Activity environments can also serve to ebb the rising tide of negative socialization by providing positive alternatives. Learning that is integrated through multisensory experience is usually more effective. In spite of this, the curriculum for young children leads to sedentary activities such as paper and pencil tasks, work books, and programed or computer assisted instruction. Is it not ludicrous to shackle young children behind desks for extended periods of time when so much can be learned through more natural, active pursuits? Turning little children into little adults in school, in sports, and in the home occurs too soon and too often in life.

Sitting still and keeping quiet is certainly not an efficient way of learning for children and is even questionable for adults who have supposedly learned to sit and listen. It is by doing and experiencing that real learning takes place, particularly in terms of psychological and social development. Behavior and values are rarely altered for extended periods of time by sitting and listening. Concepts like trust can be taught from a book or some students can shut their eyes and let others lead them around the room or even across a street. People can be told about the importance of cooperation or they can experience it. Active games are experience sessions. Due to their dynamic nature children are acting and reacting in both a physical and psychological sense.

We cannot legislate constructive play patterns, cooperation, love, security, identity, happiness, and affection. But a society that does not give all the necessary external supports to bring this about may find that it is lost in violence, juvenile delinquency, mugging, and crowded prisons. Not only is this spiritual loss, but also a heavy financial burden for all of us.[3]

Today, the human species could resurrect the cooperative values of the stone age in conditions of sufficiency rather than scarcity, and thereby eliminate any need for children to learn exaggerated competition and its extension in destructive aggression.

The best preparation for being a humanistic, responsible and happy adult is to live fully as a child. One reason that cooperative games have great potential in this regard is that the structure of the game itself should ensure a certain level of acceptance for each child and should ensure that certain desirable behaviors are reinforced.

To introduce the games is all that should be necessary. The fact that active games are in themselves rewarding for many children makes them an ideal medium from a motivational standpoint. If programs are properly constructed children will be able to engage in physical activity, learn appropriate behaviors, and have fun in the process.

Cooperative games may be of particular significance to children who are shy or withdrawn, who lack self confidence, who feel insecure, who don't feel liked, who have inadequate social skills, who have not learned to respond in a friendly manner, or who are reluctant to approach problems or people. It has been found that children who are deficient in social interaction skills are seriously handicapped in acquiring many behavioral repertoires necessary for effective social functioning. Social isolation is an extremely serious problem in North America. The basic problem is said to be a consequence of cultural norms which overemphasize competition, individual success, and personal responsibility for failure. The most effective therapy may be to understand and change cultural values.

The more insecure we feel, the more we need to feel

accepted, and the more we appreciate being liked. Elementary school-age social isolates are more often integrated into the group and accepted by peers under cooperative rather than under competitive conditions. In Aronson's cooperative classroom learning program, some teachers commented on the changes they observed, specifically citing cases of withdrawn and shy children who brightened up and were excited by school.

In our observations with 4- and 5-year-olds we see some children who are totally off on their own, never interacting with others. We see others who interact in destructive ways. One young lad recently squeezed a girl's arm until she cried, with no noticeable provocation. Another young girl hits on a regular basis and recently split another child's head open. Still another child has tantrums regularly when he doesn't get exactly what he wants the instant he wants it.

It is interesting to note that these children, who are the most aggressive and least cooperative in their kindergarten class, are the least liked by classmates. They are well on their way to a rejected existence. No one wants them as a friend. No one wants them to come on a special picnic with them. The don't have a chance simply because they have not learned appropriate cooperative behaviors. Their destructive modes of behavior could pose serious problems later in life unless replaced by more appropriate types of interaction.

Virtually every killer, every rapist, every terrorist was once a little child who played games and attended school. If we do not seize upon these opportunities to teach children about human values and let them experience the value of other people, we are missing the boat completely.

All the performance skills in the world are wasted in a misdirected performer. We must therefore shift from performance skills to human skills.

Atypical children such as the mentally retarded usually possess few, if any, appropriate play behaviors. I have personally witnessed institutionalized, emotionally disturbed children playing in a play yard. Rarely, if ever, have I seen a cooperative social interaction. But it has been found that through the positive use of imitation, prompting and reinforcement, social interaction and cooperative play behaviors can be developed in severely retarded children. These social interaction skills also generalize to other environments.

With respect to increasing the transferability of behavior from one environment to another, cooperative games to cooperative lives, some points are worthy of note. We can attempt to increase the similarity between training settings and other settings. If cooperation in games simulates the kind of cooperation to be desired in other settings as well, it is more likely to transfer.

We can have the children practice cooperating in numerous settings—in the playground, in the classroom, and in the home. We can train or encourage people in the child's natural environment to use cooperative structures and selective reinforcements for cooperative behavior in a manner similar to that followed in cooperative game sessions. We can also teach the child to manage his own behavior.

We should consider Risley's research at the University of Kansas, which demonstrates that entire classes of behavior can be developed in children by involving the youngsters in establishing groupings of behavior which they feel are desirable and appropriate. Discussion, reasoning, intermittent reinforcement, and reviewing children's current desirable behavior appear to result in the generalization of response. The active cognitive involvement required by the children seems to help the youngsters quickly learn to generalize from a specific behavior to a host of other different, but related, behaviors and situations.

If cooperative games can be used to prevent social isolation and to facilitate positive social interaction, they will be of immense value to both normal and problem children, many of whom are potentially normal.

The value of cooperating with others and the significance of fun becomes increasingly important as our society becomes increasingly competitive and technical. Where else can a child become so immersed in something so joyous and yet learn something so valuable about himself and others? Opportunities for cooperative social interaction, self acceptance, and sheer fun must be nurtured, rather than destroyed, in the games children play. Those of us concerned with overall quality of life, and more specifically with children's psychological health, must work together so that confident, cooperative, joyous children do not become an endangered species.

STRUCTURES AND ALTERNATIVE STRUCTURES

A basic structural problem exists in most present day games due to the fact that two or more people or teams are basing their feelings of success and adequacy upon something which only one can have—the scoreboard victory. This problem can lead to a host of other problems, unless victory is kept in perspective. It becomes a question of how far people will go in order to achieve the victory and how they react when they don't. Psycho-social problems usually arise when two or more individuals or groups become obsessed with achieving an end which, by the very structure of the game, can be achieved by only one. In order to alleviate these problems one must either work within this structure, and attempt to alter the single view of "victory," or attempt to alter the basic structure in some way.

To illustrate the importance of the structure of a game as well as the emphasis within a game, let's assume we were playing the game Winner on the Spot. Simply place a two-foot square, black rubber mat on the floor. Whoever is standing on the spot 30 seconds from now is the winner. Go!!! What do you think would happen?

Now let's add a few conditions to increase the importance of the outcome: Winners are smothered with praise and recognition and are paid large sums of money; losers are rejected and humiliated. What do you think people will do now in order to be winner on the spot?

Go a step further and try to make the players feel and know that their whole value as a person, their worth in life, their job, their self respect, depends upon whether they end up in that spot. Add the thought that, "If you don't get them, they will get you. They are the enemy!" Use televised games and "on the spot" heroes to help relay this message. Now what do you think players will do to be the winner? And how many losers will continue "playing?"

Now completely reverse the structure. Change the name of the game to All on the Spot. The new objective is to get as many people as possible either on the spot or touching the spot. Go!!! Now what do you think would happen? This is how a structure can influence behavior.

It should be noted that people's past experiences and attitudes can affect their behavior within structures. For example, in our original Winner on the Spot game (without the additional winning conditions), do you think that females would react the same as males in terms of what they would be willing to do in order to win? How about people from more cooperative cultures?

Clearly not all cultures and not all people within cultures are fixated on winning, even within competitive game structures. For example, Burmese children were playing basketball and the score was tied with three minutes to go. At this point one youngster walked off the court and sat down. When asked why, he said he was tired.

Competitive games in cooperative cultures don't seem to pose any great problem because winning never becomes a life and death issue. Although the game is structured competitively, the players approach it in a friendly and cooperative manner. Although individuals may strive to do the best they can, there is no shame in someone doing better, nor is there any animosity toward "opponents." This is a healthy and mutually reinforcing competition. If we were capable of maintaining this type of perspective in our competitive games and competitive lives, we would not be experiencing the problems that are now evident. Perhaps when members of our society have been socialized in a more cooperative and humanistic vein, we will be capable of playing competitive games in a friendly and jovial manner. But until that time we had better focus on alternatives.

Let's get back to the female orientation. Research has

shown that females respond more uniformly to the needs of others and are more willing to engage in sharing behavior under differing conditions. While males appear to be more oriented toward competing for personal gains, females behave more in accordance with social responsibility. If, with respect to such things as concern for others, social orientation, and empathy, males could be socialized more along the lines in which we socialize females, we would have considerably more humane games and lives.

Although females are raised in the same society and perhaps even in the same home, they are generally more concerned with the welfare of others and are not as obsessed with the outcome of a competitive game. This may relate to the tendency for females to be less competitively conditioned than their male counterparts, particularly in physical pursuits, revolving around play and games. Females may also feel that they have less at stake under game conditions. If the stakes were raised their behavior might more closely approximate male behavior. For example, if their physical or spiritual life were at stake, or the approval of their loved ones, they would probably become more intensely competitive to become the winner on the spot.

It is obvious that we already selectively socialize many responses, some of which are desirable, others not so. It is important that this effort be more concerted and more directed toward humanistic ends. Destructive orientations as well as constructive orientations are learned, as is modesty. We don't start with all these belief systems and modes of response. They occur as a result of a process of socialization. When you work with 3-, 4- and 5-year-olds this becomes blatantly obvious. The other day when we were playing some cooperative games, a beautiful little 5-year-old scooted off to the bathroom which adjoins the gym. A few moments later her little head popped through the door and she bellowed out, "There's no paper, I can't wipe my bum." The rest of the class went on playing, oblivious to her sticky plight.

On another occasion, when we were engaged in some active games, right in the middle of a game one girl threw off her dress in one full sweep. She wanted to be free to run and so she was. There's nothing inherently wrong with either of these acts yet ten years from now these youngsters will have learned to respond differently and may cringe at the thought of having behaved in this way. The simple point is that people learn "appropriate" modes of response, whether it is with respect to codes of dress or codes of competition.

Although positive socialization is one of the stated aims of many activity programs and educational experiences, little has been done in terms of constructing environments to accomplish this objective. Points, grades and other rewards have long been given for performance objectives, for scoring, for winning. However, rarely have reinforcements been made (dependent) upon social objectives and desirable person-to-person human interaction. In fact, there is little reason to be helpful and cooperative under many of our present reward structures. There are often reasons not to be helpful. Thus, the choice to cooperate is essentially eliminated.

In order to work within contemporary win-loss structures, to bring about change, we must reduce the participants' perception of the importance of the numerical outcome and provide different criteria for acceptance and success. An alternative to this lies in providing new kinds of win-win structures which lead to games without losers.

Where new approaches or new structures have been put forth, we have attempted in our games to guarantee full participation, to ensure feelings of acceptance and fun, to develop positive interpersonal values, and to promote cooperation. We have tried to help set the stage so that children learn to value other children and come to recognize that personal victories are not necessarily dependent upon others' defeat. We have attempted to help children realize that everyone playing a game, everyone on a team, everyone in a gym class is an integral part of it. We have introduced rules to help bring this about. Once these basic values have been well learned and accepted, rules to this effect are often no longer necessary.

By introducing activities and games which alter the contemporary win-loss concept, a person's original desire to play for the intrinsic values of the game is legitimized and rekindled. This in turn provides a meaningful niche for the masses of our people, young and old, in the realm of active involvement. For the youngster who later chooses to pursue the route of excellence, having been exposed to cooperative games, he or she should be capable of approaching competition and team cooperation in a healthy and positive way.

Experience in new games should demonstrate that acceptance as a human being is not totally dependent upon a score. Consequently for those who wish, sports could become a quest to develop oneself without becoming an attempt to destroy others and without becoming a fearsome, life and death issue.

Children's initial exposures to cooperative games can

be enhanced by increasing the attractiveness of the activity, the attractiveness of the potential cooperators, the attractiveness of the rewards associated with cooperating, and the immediacy with which cooperation leads to the desired goal. It should be remembered that in a competitive society an individual's perception of the effectiveness and attractiveness of a cooperative solution may have been blurred by his socialization into competitive solutions for everything. Successful cooperative experiences during childhood will help to crystalize the attractiveness of cooperative alternatives throughout life.

THE FOCUS FOR CHANGE

In our quest for positive change one strategy would be to focus on adult behavior in hopes that teachers, coaches, parents, and other adults will set appropriate examples, and relay cooperative, humanistic values. Significant people in a child's life certainly have the potential to influence value structures, self perceptions, and behaviors. However, to follow this route we must first change the behavior of the adult, who must in turn attempt to influence the child's behavior. As we are all aware, changing adult behavior is no easy task, and, when we then expect these adults to act upon this newly acquired behavior, in order to influence others in their charge, the task becomes even more difficult.

By increasing the degree of commitment, we can increase the consistency between our words and deeds. Commitment is defined as the pledging or binding of an individual to behavioral acts. The degree of commitment in physical activity settings could be increased by:

1. Increasing the explicitness of an intention (i.e., increasing its publicness and specificity)
2. Increasing the responsibility for the behavior (i.e., perceived importance and perceived freedom in stating the intention)
3. Periodically reviewing stated goals and intentions (i.e., frequent reminders and restatements of intention).

Cal Botterill, who is presently working with the Coaching Association of Canada, put these hypotheses to test in an applied situation with different sports teams. On one occasion he put up the following notice: Anyone Who Wants To Play Hockey Who Has Not Made A Team— Report To The Arena At 3:30 on Tuesday. Fifteen 10- to 13-year old boys who had been cut from other teams showed up. A series of discussions were held whereby they began to set their own goals and objectives for the year. Botterill posed questions relating to why the boys wanted to play hockey this year, what they wanted to accomplish, and how they might go about doing it. For example, if they wanted to have fun or improve, what suggestions did they have to bring this about? They were also asked to think about why certain kinds of behaviors, for example passing or helping, might be better than others, such as hogging or fighting. The players talked things over and reached a consensus, sometimes through voting. Once there was agreement, the team's basic objectives were distributed to the parents. The boys agreed upon an equal play, equal time rule and there was no "static" about this from *any* parents, primarily because the players had set the rule.

The Eagles, as they came to be know, lost their first game 20-0. When a hockey team loses a game 20-0, it's tough to find much to praise. However, by the use of specific short term goals relating to various behaviors and skills, such as knowing where to be on the ice, being able to turn both ways, not getting penalties, Botterill pointed out some legitimate areas of improvement. In practice, the players created some of their own drills. They came up with some unique fun drills, one of which was free skating across the rink, one by one, doing anything you could imagine, like hot dog skiing. They loved it!

By the middle of the season the team was "losing" by 12-4, better than last week. As the season moved toward a close, the Eagles finally did it, they accomplished one of their long term goals, they won a game—Eagles 2-Visitors 1. All hell broke loose and all 15 boys who began the season were there to enjoy it. The Eagles had won! This was partially a result of the vast improvements the boys had made and partially a result of Botterill's ability to find weaker teams to play. A few years after the Eagles' debut, Botterill returned to the area where he had taught and coached and was pleased to find that a large percentage of these same youngsters were still playing hockey.

Botterill also coached a team comprised of some of the most skilled boys in the league to the city championship, using a democratic self control approach. The team began by democratically coming up with an agreement or consensus about the group's objectives and the best way to achieve them. They set goals under the following categories which were provided by the coach: Behavior as a team member, with fans, with parents, with coach, with officials, with teammates, toward opponents, fun goals, fitness goals, team goals, individual goals. If a truly cooperative motivational climate is established, stated goals and intentions tend to be socially desirable and normative. This was certainly the case here as Botterill found that his teams consistently set tougher and more desirable goals than he had for them.

The team members not only decided what was desirable and what was not, but also set the consequences for inappropriate behavior. If you complained to a teammate or argued with an official, you'd miss the next shift on the ice. If you did it again you'd miss the rest of the game. Within a short period of time, the number of inappropriate offenses declined dramatically and if an offense was committed, the player recognized it as inappropriate and would automatically sit out a shift on his own. No one had to tell him.

Once realistic objectives are clearly outlined and agreed upon, there tends to be more consistent encouragement and reinforcement of desirable behavior by peers, and peer group sanctions have great impact. Behaviors such as arguing with officials, complaining to teammates, tardiness, cheating, destructive aggression, can all be quickly eliminated if declared inconsistent with the team goals. In addition, the moral charge of manipulation which is often directed at behavior modification is substantially weakened when the behavioral goals are democratically conceived by the group. You simply "encourage and reinforce behavior which is consistent with specified goals and expectations, and discourage, fail to acknowledge, or punish behavior which is inconsistent with what has been decided," reports Botterill. In summary, Botterill has found that involving the boys in the overall planning and specific goal setting helps to clarify goals, eliminate problem behavior, improve motivation, increase commitment, and promote the feeling that it is *their* team.

The local minor hockey association in Estevan, Saskatchewan, headed by junior high school principal Bernard Collins, attempted to "educate" adults into behaving more appropriately at games. Before each game, the following announcement was read by a member of the minor hockey association: "LADIES AND GENTLEMEN: The following are a few points the EMHA would like to suggest so that you, the fans, the officials, and teams may better enjoy the game you're about to see:

1. The officials of this game know and respect the rules. The EMHA expects players, coaches and fans to respect the officials.
2. Should you have any comments to make, please make them to the proper officials of EMHA at the proper time (not during the game).
3. Verbal abuse toward any players, coach or official will *not* be tolerated. Anyone doing so will be asked to leave the rink immediately.
4. Unsportsmanlike behavior by anyone participating in the game will be dealt with severely by the EMHA.
5. If you can offer your services in this or any other game in Minor Hockey, please notify the coaches or any EMHA official.
6. Your attendance at this game is appreciated by players, coaches and officials. Enjoy it and "Make hockey FUN for them!"

Some of the above strategies have the potential to stimulate positive change and should certainly be commended. However, in the long run it may be easier to change the games than to change the adults. It may be more fruitful to introduce new games than to change old orientations. We may come closer to achieving our objectives if we simply let cooperative games do the shaping rather than relying upon people who have been conditioned toward traditional winning ways. How many Botterills do we have among the coaching ranks? This is not to suggest that we forget about working towards appropriate adult input, but it does suggest that we must explore other alternatives. We simply cannot rely on many of our present adult models and adult reinforcements to effect the kinds of changes I am talking about.

It is questionable whether much lasting behavior change takes place as a result of simple discourse, reading, clinics, conferences, and so on. First of all, many of those who most need to change do not attend these workshops, and, even if they do attend, verbalization is not likely to have a great deal of impact on those with a history of reinforcement for behaving in a contrary manner. Verbalization, reading, and clinics may help set the stage for some reflection but certainly do not guarantee any behavioral change. Enduring changes in behavior take place in the natural environment, through everyday interactions with people.

Games are one important element of the natural environment, as is the home, the community and the school. If adults begin to encourage cooperative game objectives as they now do with competitive game objectives, then the games have the potential of shaping not only the children but also the adults. They have the potential to help close the gap between adults' stated attitudes and their overt behavior, between what children say they want and what they now get. In addition, reward structures can be changed in children's games without changing reward structures in society. It is therefore feasible to introduce behaviors and values through play and games which may in time affect society as a whole.

IN THE BEGINNING

The exciting thing about new games is that they allow you to start over again. They give you the opportunity to start with nothing and create something. I remember when we first started playing some of our cooperative games at a summer camp in Ottawa. I looked down to the other end of the field and saw between 20 and 25 nine-year-olds, half of whom were sitting on a bench and the other half of whom were scattered around the field, standing motionless. Only two or three people seemed to be moving. One was throwing a small object toward another who was swinging something wooden through the air. Swoosh, swoosh, swoosh . . . followed by another individual taking the wooden object and beginning a series of swooshes. Occasionally a child would make contact with a small round object which stirred the action of two or three more children.

I began to wonder what would happen if this game I was watching was a new and unknown game, which I was trying to introduce for the first time, rather than the well established game of baseball. Would the children agree to be so inactive or to sit for such a long period of time only to swoosh through the air. What would the children feel like if they were one of the many who never made contact with the ball either at bat or in the field. Would the game be "fun"? When analyzed in this light the game appears to have very little to offer young children, yet the game is widely accepted. It is accepted because children have been socialized into accepting it by a society which has known the game for many years.

Perhaps an even better example is American tackle football. If for the first time you lined up children and told them to smash into each other in order to bring a little oval shaped object to the other side of the field, how many would immediately accept it and how many would benefit from it? Amazingly enough, children are conditioned into accepting it and some even learned to enjoy smashing other people into the ground. With repeated exposure in the community, in school, in the park, and on television, certain games have come to be accepted even though they may have started with very few positive components for children. This may be an important point to keep in mind when introducing cooperative games, especially when we know that they are appropriately designed for children.

---

[1]G.B. Leonard on "Winning Isn't Everything: It's Nothing," in *Intellectual Digest*, October 1973. See bibliography.

[2]See Sax and Hollonder, *Reality Games* in bibliography.

[3]See B. Ward "Children—An Endangered Species" in bibliography.

Contemporary Cooperative Games

An interesting comparison which was made between formal acting and creative dramatics may have some significance in helping to distinguish between formal athletics and cooperative games:

> Theatre develops actors, creative dramatics develops people. In fact the more formal stage play might well damage the self confidence which creative dramatics is trying to strengthen. Further, the presence of an audience only interferes with the imaginative, sensitive involvement of successful creative drama. Few children are natural actors, but everyone can be 100 percent successful in creative drama.[1]

The primary objective of cooperative games is to provide opportunities for cooperative learning and fun-filled cooperative interaction. As was pointed out earlier, merely bringing competitively socialized people together in small groups is not sufficient to enhance cooperation or liking. The people must be linked together in some interdependent way; the structure of the activity sets the conditions for interdependence.

Some sports already elicit a great amount of

cooperative interdependence among team members. For example, volleyball played by skilled participants involves many set-ups and bumps to fellow team members. In rowing, members of a crew have to work together to make the shell move efficiently. In pairs skating the interdependent link is obvious in both process and outcome. Activities or situations which elicit the greatest amount of cooperation with the least amount of conflict, bitterness, or putting down of other people, would seem best for constructive cooperative learning and mutual liking. For activities like those mentioned above which elicit cooperation within each team, it is possible to rotate the team membership in order to create new interdependent relationships. This should result in an increased level of liking within the entire group of people (e.g., members of all or both teams) and should help ensure that the numerical outcomes do not become more important than people's welfare. If in the bigger games of life and death, such as political games, money games, and war games, players became interdependently linked with the other side, they would probably begin to understand, accept and empathize with the previous "enemy." If it were possible to implement this on a broad scale, human compassion and trust might result.

An alternative to switching sides or rotating team members is to establish overriding goals which are real and compelling to all concerned. In order to encourage members of opposing teams to cooperate, common goals can be established within games which are attractive to both sides. This method is similar to the approach followed by Sherif to encourage hostile camp groups to cooperate in that the goals are constructed so that they can only be achieved with the cooperation of the members of the group.

Initially it is difficult to think up stimulating cooperative activities and noncompetitive games which have no losers. Perhaps this is a result of the overall orientation of our society which limits our cooperative experiences and narrows our vision of games and sports. However, we have found that once you get into the cooperative swing of things, cooperative ideas are generated rather quickly and regularly.

Following are some cooperative ideas translated into action, which will hopefully serve as a stimulus to many more new alternatives. The cooperative games presented in this book should be viewed as the beginning of a new era rather than as something firm and final. They represent the beginning of greater opportunity games, of games without physical or psychological violations.

A few samples of various types of cooperative games are provided under the categories: cooperative games with no losers, collective score games, reversal games, and semi-cooperative games. A wealth of additional cooperative games are presented in my *Cooperative Sports and Games Book*. It is my sincere hope that you will draw upon the games presented, play with them, expand them, adapt them, and by all means use the concept behind them.

COOPERATIVE GAMES WITH NO LOSERS

Cooperative Musical Chairs: In the normal game of musical chairs, every child starts sitting in a chair. When the music begins the children skip around the room and one chair is removed from the playing area. When the music stops the children scramble to find a chair for themselves and one child is forced out because he no longer has a chair. This chair removal process continues until all but one child is eliminated. If 21 children play, you are guaranteed that 20 will be losers. Only one child will be a winner. This is a game of elimination, similar to many other contemporary games. Its structure elicits competition and demands elimination. It is hard for many children to feel really involved in this type of game and even more difficult for them to like someone who just shoved them out of their chair.

In the game of *Cooperation Musical Chairs* the object is to keep every child in the game, even though chairs are being removed. As each chair is removed more children have to team together sitting on parts of chairs, or on top of one another, to keep everyone in. Instead of fighting for the sole possession of one chair, children work together to make themselves part of it. To move the game along, begin with enough chairs for half the group which means they start out with two on a chair. The game generally ends when one or two chairs are left with everyone precariously perched on one another. A five-year-old girl once suggested that we continue to play until no chairs were left. We tried it and it worked. Twenty-one children were all lumped happily together atop an imaginary chair.

Observations: high degree of active involvement; high degree of cooperation; high level of enjoyment for kindergarten, and grade 1, and adults.

Log Roll or Laughing Logs: Six or more players (logs) lie next to one another on their stomachs on the floor. One player lies on his stomach across the upper part of their backs. All the logs begin rolling in the same direction giving one player (the rider) a ride across the top of the logs. When the rider reaches the other side he becomes the first rolling log, and the last log becomes the rider. This continues all the way across the room, gym or field. I had originally called the game giant log roll but a five-year-old boy informed me that they were really laughing logs. It is a good game to try at a party, although not everyone rolls on their first date.

Observations: high degree of active involvement; high degree of cooperation; high level of enjoyment for all age groups.

Giant Potato Sac or All in the Sac: We made a gigantic potato sac that a whole class can fit into if they cooperate. The children are asked to get in the sac (first in small groups) to see if they can move the sac from one point to another. Coordinated crawling, rolling or jumping can move the sac. This activity was not only successful with young children but also with older age groups. For example, when we played All in the Sac with my university class, one person commented, "Fantastic, I've been trying to get into the sac with her all year. I finally did it."

Observations: high degree of active involvement; high degree of cooperation; high level of enjoyment for all age groups.

COLLECTIVE SCORE GAMES

We have played a variety of different types of collective score or collective goal games with different age groups. These games tend to break down the traditional barriers of one team playing *against* another. The games are generally quite active and incorporate the concept of teams working toward one common goal or score without competing against others. For games which involve volleying skills, balloons are often used with the younger children and beach balls are used with the older ones to increase the chances of "success." For some games we use light rubber, canvas covered "cageballs," "pushballs," "monsterballs," "earthballs" or weather balloons which are between 3 and 20 times as large as a beach ball. If a monsterball is not available we simply throw a bunch of beach balls into a big sack. The examples of collective score games outlined below have generally been received enthusiastically by different age groups and by both sexes.

Collective Score Blanketball: This game· is played by two separate teams attempting to toss a beach ball or monsterball back and forth over a volleyball net, using a blanket. Each team, comprised of approximately ten players, is provided with a blanket and can only use the blanket as a means of propelling the ball. Every time the ball is tossed over the net by one team and caught successfully by the other team, a collective point is scored. Collective points are accumulated in this manner until the ball hits the floor, at which time the counting begins over again. If a team tosses the ball and it does not go over the net, they try to catch it before it hits the ground, then they try again. This game is extremely cooperative as every team member is a part of every toss and every catch made by his or her team. In addition both teams are working together toward a common end. The size of the blanket, the type of ball, the number of blankets, the number of balls, and the number of players per side are all very adaptable. The sides do not have to be equal and players can come and go if they please. Structually it is a very well conceived game and it's lots of fun. Definitely no losers!

Bump and Scoot: The game begins with two teams of about seven players each on different sides of a volleyball net. Whenever a person on one team hits the beach ball over the net, he scoots under the net to the other side. Players attempt to make a complete change in teams with as few drops of the ball as possible, or without dropping the ball. This is an active game that the children really like and we have found it is a good way to integrate boys and girls. In fourth and fifth grades, if the boys do not want to be on the same team as the girls, the boys can start on one side of the net and the girls can start on the other. They share a *common end*, become members of the same team, and "feed" one another in order to enable all team members to move to the other side.

REVERSAL GAMES

Reversal games really play with our traditional concept of winning and losing. The games leave most players feeling they have won or uncertain as to whether they have won. I have yet to have anyone tell me they lost. Our rigid concept of teams is broken down as players become rotating members of both teams. The reversal approach seems to reduce the exaggerated concern about score, as numerical outcome and sides are no longer clear cut. Your team may have the most points but the other team may have given you the points, and in addition you may have been on their team for 5 or 10 minutes. You are not likely to attribute your reason for playing solely to winning, when points and "opponents" are played with in this manner. In a sense you're really just one big team helping each other to enjoy the activity and process of the game. These games are sure to get a very interesting, if not always a totally accepting response.

The first reversal games presented, which involve the rotation of players between teams, are relatively conservative when compared with the score reversal games. The most radical departure from tradition is the concept of Total Reversal. I am attempting to prepare you for it. Remember, keep an open mind.

Rotational Volleyball: This game is similar to regular volleyball but instead of rotating within the team, the rotation of players includes both teams. Once a server from both teams has relinquished the service they move to the middle of the back line of the *other* team. Their new position places them last in line to become server on their new team. It is difficult to get mad at the other team or to lose to the other team, as you are or will be on the other team at some point in time. This same concept can be used in other contemporary games by having entire offensive and defensive teams change sides as new shifts of players come on the field or ice.

Reverse Scorer: In this game the scorer switches to the other team immediately after scoring, if the other team is losing. No one from the other team is exchanged. The team that scores gets the point but the scorer goes to the "losing" team. If desired the scorer may switch only if the other team is down by a few points. Reversing scorer can be accomplished with no stoppage in play, the scorer merely switches sides or shifts while the game continues. This can be used for football, hockey, soccer, etc.

Reverse Score: This game resembles a regular game but the points made go to the other team. The objective is to give the other team as many gifts, or points, as possible. In order to give them a point you score on them.

Total Reversal: In this game there is no goalie, points go to the other team, and scorers switch to the "winning" team, which is the team with the most points, but actually the weakest team because it got its points by being scored upon.

By now you're probably asking yourself, where the hell did this guy come up with these games? I must admit I can't take credit for this reversal concept. The idea came from an eight-year-old boy whom I had the pleasure of interviewing. The exchange went as follows:

Terry: How could you change sports to make them better or more fun?

Boy: You could do it backwards.

Terry: What do you mean?

Boy: Well, like if the other team gets a goal, then you get the points, and then if we get a goal, they get a goal. Like we're not really getting a goal, they are. We try to make a goal for them and they try to make a goal for us.

Terry: Why do you think that would be better?

Boy: Cause it would help 'em like each other better.

Initially the game of broomball was played with a group of northern Indian children to test out this child's "do it backwards" suggestion. The first time we introduced the new version of the game to the seventh and eighth grade students there were no goalies and two unique rules were introduced: 1) Each goal your team gets is a gift to the other team. If you get the goal they get the point. 2) The person who scores the goal gets to be on the team with the most points (actually the weakest team). If you score and your team has the most points you stay on the same team but if the other team has the most points then you change teams.

The northern children cooperated right from the start. Although they didn't understand the implications of the rule changes they were quite willing to play and find out what would happen. It was obvious from the first few minutes of play that the teams were uneven in ability. However, after the strongest team had scored three goals, three players had moved to the weaker team, which then began to score. Once the score was even again there was a tendency for it to stay near a tie.

After several goals had been scored the players began to realize what was happening but they didn't have much time to figure out what their strategy should be. At this point some of the more assertive players held back from the play but gradually got back into it when they realized that the individual who scored would always become a member of the team with the most points, although if he did change teams it was always to the weaker team. Thus there were pros and cons to scoring. Once they realized this they all began to try to score again. This was particularly evident on penalty shots because there was no goalie. At one time, the penalty shooters were obviously not trying to score but before long the strategy changed and they began trying again.

The final score became less important to the individual players because of the way the rigid team structure was broken down. Possibly as a result of this, the players used less body checking and "hacky" play. They played the ball more. As a result of not having a goalie, there tended to be more scoring than in their normal broomball games, thus providing more opportunities for success experiences. Perhaps the most significant event occurred at the end of the game when the teacher announced that the winners were to take the brooms back into the school. Nearly everyone took in a broom.

It is significant that the children played the game and cooperated to the extent that they tried to score even when the point was going to the other team but the scorer was not going to the other team, since his own team had more points. Based on a questionnaire evaluation of the game, there appeared to be very good acceptance of the new rules by the girls and moderate acceptance by the boys.

This all sounds very nice but when we repeated the game with a group of seventh and eighth grade children in Ottawa, the initial response was markedly different. Immediately after the new rules were introduced to the children, remarks such as, "That won't work," "What's the point of the game?" and "How do you win?" were voiced openly by several of the boys. In spite of their reservations concerning the value of such a game, they agreed to try it. After five minutes of play, the yellow team had been scored upon three times and consequently was ahead by three points and had three extra players. Within minutes the yellow team scored twice to even out the score somewhat. As the game progressed the yellow team again went ahead by three points, having had been scored upon three more times. At this time (i.e., having a several point advantage and a few additional players), some players on the yellow team began to stand around rather thay play the ball. Two boys on this team went so far as to try to score on their own goal so that they would get additional points. (If this happens you can let it ride and see what happens, or introduce a rule which states that no points count for scoring on your own goal, or tell the other team that they can protect the other team's goal.) It is interesting that these children seemed to perceive the team with the most points as the "winning" team, even though points were given to the team when it was scored upon, and it was actually the weaker team.

Some of the better players scored three or four times and were alternating teams regularly. One of them said that he did not know which team he was really on. Another child remarked that each person would only play for himself since only he could benefit from scoring a goal (apparently because he alone could go to the winning team, that is, the weakest team). It should be noted that many of the girls seemed to enjoy the game. However, some of the more competitive boys seemed to feel that because the game did not offer one team or individual a chance to win in a more customary manner, it was "a waste of time."

When we compare these observations to those of the northern children, the extent to which competitive game socialization has taken hold in southern Canada by 13 years of age becomes apparent. The northern children's receptivity to this reversal concept seems to demonstrate their greater willingness to cooperate and share. Perhaps it also indicates an acceptance of playing for fun, and an ability to focus on the process rather than the outcome.

It should be noted that total reversal broomball was played on only one occasion with each of the above groups. Since that time we have played reversal games with different age groups, in different sports, and more than once with the same group. When total reversal broomball was played with a group of 9- and 10-year old Ottawa children, they were much more receptive than their 13-year-old peers.

I observed a game of floor hockey being played by eight-year-olds with reverse score only, and the level of acceptance was even more evident. The teams tried hard even though the score went to the other side and they really had fun playing. A boy on the red team moved up, shot and scored. He cheered! At the same instant a youngster on the "opposing" team also cheered. At the end of the game the final score was 6-4.

Both teams charged into the change room yelling, "We won . . . we won."

"No, we won . . . because you got the most points on us."

One girl in grade three told her teacher, "It was fun" playing floor hockey with the new rules because "Everyone won, since there was switching. We scored and they got the point."

We have found that total reversal is often too dramatic a change to introduce as an initial exposure to the reversal concept with seasoned players, even though rookies may be able to handle it. Therefore we generally first have the children play their regular game and only change one thing, such as reversing the score. We try not to complicate things by also switching teams and playing with no goalie. Each of these concepts can be introduced one at a time and if desired combined at a later date.

SEMI-COOPERATIVE GAMES

After all that "far out" reversal stuff here is something for the more traditional at heart. The most traditional alternatives we have attempted maintain the basic structure of the game but attempt to alter the emphasis within the game. One team still plays against another team but the importance of the scoreboard outcome is downplayed. Instead the emphasis is placed on active involvement and having fun. All people are given equal opportunities to play regardless of age, sex or ability. Adjustments are made in equipment, rules and feedback to enable more success, to maximize· activity, and to curb undesirable or destructive behavior. Sincere attempts are made to minimize negative experiences, to avoid situations of embarrassment, and to eliminate feelings of rejection. An attempt is made to keep the teams even (by shifting players from "opposing" teams if necessary) and the same leader, if there is one, may be responsible for two "opposing" teams (i.e., players on team A and players on team B). We often play traditional games without keeping score and without officials which is an attempt to reinforce the idea that you really can play for fun and be responsible for your own behavior without overconcern with the scoreboard.

In order to ensure that every player feels a part of the action we have attempted to introduce rules to this effect. When you sit down and count the number of times each team member touches the ball or puck in a community game or in a gym class, you find that some never touch the ball while others dominate the action.

I watched a fourth grade class play floor hockey for

half a gym period and there was virtually no passing. There was no cooperation even within teams. They fought with their teammates to get the ball and then blasted it in the general direction of the goal. With the following rule changes, we have increased cooperation among team members and have given participants the opportunity to play different positions. These rule changes are extremely effective in integrating everyone into the action.

All Play: Everyone who wants to play is given equal playing time. Attempts are made to keep teams small enough for everyone to play all of the allocated activity time.

All Touch/All Pass: A regular game but before a shot is attempted, the ball or puck is passed to and touched by all members of the team. Once a point is scored the ball is again passed to all team members before another shot is taken. Good for soccer, frisbee soccer, hockey, water polo, scooter ball, anything.

All Score: A regular game in which, for one team to win, each team member must score at least once. Can be played with large goals, for example the whole end of a gym, rink or pool. Once every member of one team scores, a new game is started. If there is any evidence of unwanted pressure being placed on those last to score, which we have not yet experienced, discuss the problem among the players. They may decide to adjust their tactics or might want to consider introducing four-score in place of All Score.

Both All Pass and All Score set up a cooperative situation *within the team* where teammates "feed" to one another to achieve the objective of the game. These rules also allow each child to feel important and give everyone an opportunity to improve their skills.

Coed Pass: A regular game in which the ball or puck is passed alternatively from female to male to female, etc.

Coed Score: A regular game in which goals are scored alternatively by males and females. An interesting variation is a rule which states that a male and female must be holding hands for either to score. The acceptability of these coed rules depends upon the age and maturity of the group. However at any age Coed Pass and Coed Score serve to integrate both males and females into the action.

All Positions: Players rotate through the various positions during the period of the game. This can be done on the basis of time, score or inning. For example, positions may be switched after three minutes of play, after three downs, after each score, or at the end of each inning. Position rotation can be used in soccer, football, baseball, or hockey, etc., much as it now occurs in volleyball. Players can also take turns, facing off, jumping ball, taking a ball out, running the ball. A modified form of all positions has been used successfully in little league football. During the course of each game every child plays three different positions, at least one of which allows him to handle the ball. This ensures that every child gets a chance in every game to throw the football, run with it, or catch it.

A group of neighborhood children ages 10 to 12 years made some additional semi-cooperative adaptations to come up with a special brand of touch "street football." They decided that each side had four downs to go from lamp-post to lamp-post (instead of only 10 yards). This resulted in the ball being turned over frequently and kept both teams interested. They made every player eligible to do everything. They instituted "passball" which allowed any player to pass the ball anyplace on the field, even beyond the line of scrimmage. Due to this rule (or nonrule) there was lots of scoring which kept the game alive. In addition *every player* took a regular turn at quarterback for four downs.

Position rotation and flexible rules are also effective in coed touch football as it ensures that females as well as males become quarterbacks, halfbacks and receivers. It also helps make the game more fun. When we played rotational broomball (rotating offense and defense) with 9-, 10- and 11-year-olds, their liking for the game immediately increased.

ACCEPTANCE OF COOPERATIVE GAMES

Based upon our observations of cooperative games played thus far, collective score games, cooperative games with no losers, and semi-cooperative games are readily acceptable to most age groups, whereas reverse score games are not as readily acceptable, particularly in their initial stages of introduction. An important point to keep in mind when introducing any of the cooperative activities is to adapt the task so that it is appropriately challenging for a particular group or individual.

At this point games which center around a collective task or collective score probably have the greatest chance of meeting our overall objectives. In these activities everyone has the sensation of gaining something, by their own contribution as well as by the contribution of all the other players. Players are truly working together for a common goal which involves all participants, on all sides. When everyone can gain from each person's contribution, a strange thing happens. People begin to help one another.

Semi-cooperative games, while still maintaining a competitive structure, are superior to traditionally competitive games because they are more cooperative and tie everyone into the action. In reverse score games there is sometimes a sense of giving away something that has been earned. Although one team has the joy of scoring, the other team has the joy of getting the point. This is often not readily acceptable in our culture. Instead of everyone feeling that everyone has gained something by the point as with collective score games, the team that scores sometimes feels that they gained something but they also lost something. Perhaps some feel that they could have gained more by not giving away the point. At any rate, even though both teams leave the game thinking they have won, the reaction is not always positive.

As a result of playing various kinds of games with children over the past few years, it has become very evident that the younger the group the less competitive they are. For example, most four- and five-year-olds are totally unconcerned with any kind of score (competitive or collective). All they want to do is play the game and when the action is finished, that's it. The score is irrelevant, it's the doing that counts. We have found young children to be most receptive to cooperative ventures and cooperative challenges. The younger the child, the less time he has had in the competitive mainstream of our society and therefore the more willing he is to accept cooperative games.

We have found females at all grade levels to be less competitive and less physically aggressive than their male counterparts. Females are more receptive to cooperative games at all ages, with the possible exception of 4- and 5-

year-olds where boys and girls are usually equally enthusiastic. This is probably a result of the selective sex role socialization which goes on in our own culture with respect to the acceptability of physically competitive pursuits for males and females. Males are "supposed to be" more competitive, females more cooperative, and so they are in the games. We have also found that children from more cooperative cultures are more receptive to cooperative games than are children from more competitive cultures. Cooperative cultures expect and reinforce more cooperative behavior both in and out of play settings, therefore there is more reason to accept cooperative games and lifestyles.

Participants in cooperative games seem to have a feeling of involvement and a sense of helping and happiness while playing the games. Following a ten-week exposure to cooperative games, questionnaires were distributed to a group of children in third, fourth, and fifth grades. All of the girls and over 80 percent of the boys surveyed felt like they were helping each other when playing cooperative games. Reasons for this feeling included, "I'm making someone happy," "Scores are higher," "Nobody wins and nobody loses," "You are just playing to have fun," "You work as a team," "You teach each other to play fair." All of the females and 90 percent of the males also indicated that they usually felt "really happy" or "happy" when playing cooperative games. Given the choice, two thirds of the 9- and 10-year-old boys and all of the girls would prefer to play games where neither side loses rather than games where one side wins and the other side loses.

The main reasons children gave for preferring no-loser games included, "More fun when everyone is working together," "You won't feel so bad cause you lost," "I usually get a turn," "Everyone participates," "It's nice to help people." The main reasons for some boys perferring games with winners and losers included, "I like to beat others," "I like to see how I do against others," "I like the challenge." These needs can be satisfied through semi-cooperative games.

The initial degree of acceptance or rejection of cooperative games, particularly reverse score games, appears to reflect the degree of conditioning to a competitive or winning ethic. This conditioning is not immutable, as we have found that those cooperative games which have more than novelty to stand on become more acceptable with repeated exposure, as is often the case with more traditional games. The structure of the environment holds the key to cooperative change just as the environment holds the key to one's initial acceptance of cooperative alternatives. Cooperative acceptance is clearly a function of the social environment. The greater the proportion of a child's total life that revolves around cooperation, and the less that it revolves around competition, the more acceptable cooperation becomes, and the more one becomes willing to cooperate in games and life. Exposure to positive cooperative models, cooperative expectancies, cooperative game structures, and other positive or successful cooperative experiences results in more cooperation.

---

[1] See Davis, Helfert and Shapiro in bibliography.

Impact of
Cooperative
Games

It is clear that high degrees of cooperation, involvement and enjoyment can be attained through cooperative games designed for this purpose. There is also evidence of increased cooperative behavior during free play in the gym and in the classroom after exposure to a cooperative games program. Prior to one of our cooperative games programs, we observed a large group of first and second grade students during free play in the gym and recorded an average of less than two incidences of cooperative behavior per 30-second observation scan. The same few children were observed cooperating on different time scans. After eight weeks of cooperative games we observed the same group with the same equipment available, over the same period of free play time and recorded an average of slightly over eight incidences of cooperative behavior per 30-second scan. The children cooperating varied throughout the observation period. This increase in cooperative behavior was not apparent with a comparison group which tended to get more competitive as the year progressed.

After being exposed to a 14-week cooperative games program, preschool children engaged in three times as much cooperative behavior during "free play" in the gym and in over twice as much cooperative behavior in a "playroom," as did a comparison group from the same nursery school that had not experienced cooperative games.

During one observation session, within a period of one minute, nine of the ten children were involved in some cooperative act. Two boys tossed a beach ball back and forth while seven other children teamed together inside one hula hoop. This particular play pattern broke up quickly, as the children began linking hands and running in groups of two, three, or four. Human hugs were a common occurrence. The gym was literally flowing with acts of togetherness. It was quite a contrast from our observations 3½ months earlier when we rarely viewed a spontaneous cooperative act and even had initial difficulty directing some cooperative acts. Rigorous behavior observations also revealed that the rate of cooperative behavior during free play in the classroom rose substantially among kindergarten children after exposure to an 18 week co-op games program. This rise in cooperative social interaction was not seen in other kindergarten children in the same school who were exposed to a traditional games program (control groups). It is noteworthy that our trained observers were unaware of the type of program to which each group was being exposed.

When these observations are coupled with informal observations of cooperative events which kept popping up during our various games programs, it appears that something cooperative was happening both in and out of the gym. For example, after being exposed to seven hours of cooperative games, some kindergarten children were asked to make an animal with two or more in a group. A group of seven started to make a horse with their bodies but there seemed to be two extra people. Without delay they decided to make an octopus so everyone could play a part.

A five-year-old told us he was teaching the games to some little children near his home. Unfortunately, he said, they weren't very cooperative.

That same day a reporter came in to write a story about our program. He was somewhat skeptical about the whole thing at first but by the time he left he was quite excited and told me he had really changed his opinion about the entire realm of co-op games. One reason for his change of opinion was observing the kindergarteners play cooperative musical chairs and beach ball balance. For the beach ball game the children were asked to get in groups of three and to try to carry a beach ball around without using their hands. A couple of them went over to the reporter, nudged him by the hand, and said, "You can play with us." No one was playing with him and they wanted to make sure everyone had some playmates.

On another occasion after asking about the origin of our games, a five-year-old child said, "I wish they'd write those games down for my mom."

In one school, after several months of cooperative games, the teaching vice-principal noticed his fifth grade students using words like cooperation and total participation. He felt that the teachers were also doing this and incorporating these ideas into the classroom.

The boys and girls in his class began to interact more. "They mix really well now," he said, and do group work in the classroom without dividing into groups of boys and girls. Perhaps more important, he felt that his own attitude had changed. He had always been "super competitive" and involved in sports where he'd had to make the team and win or be a "failure." He felt that he was now more conscious of making sure that everyone participates, and of alternative ways of winning.

A group of special education children in this same school, aged six to nine years, were exposed to a cooperative games program from one to three times per week for a period of four months. On the days the children had cooperative games they called it their "good day." When integrating cooperative games with the learning of academic skills and perceptual motor skills, the special education teacher commented, "It really works." This was partially due to the children's obvious increased attention span resulting from a high level of interest in the activities. Within a month after the program started, the teacher began to notice a limited degree of increased cooperation in the classroom. Before each co-op games class the children collected the materials needed and returned them after class in a cooperative manner. For example, two children might roll up a number sheet or mat and carry it together. She also noted that the children were beginning to cooperate more with parent volunteers.

During the fourth month of the program there were noticeable gains in cooperation and social interaction. Generally, the children were more willing to offer assistance with assembling and dismantling equipment. And the discipline problems diminished. One child, who had lacked the ability to make close contact with others, started to communicate verbally and physically with his peers. He actually put his arm around another child and hugged him.

At that point the teacher commented, "I have never seen him show such warmth and affection."

One probable spin-off effect of the cooperative games program was the fact that half way through the program, four of the eight children in this class enrolled in a YMCA gym program. This was a "first" since none of them had ever belonged to a sports group before. The teacher felt this "new first" was due to "the added confidence gained this year in gym." At the close of the school year all four were still involved in the YMCA program.

Another spin-off effect was the positive manner in which the games influenced the teacher's personal and professional attitudes. She had continued on with the cooperative ventures and, I might add, has come up with some excellent ideas of her own. She is convinced that cooperative games are particularly well suited for special education children, for children who are frustrated and come out second best in competitive situations, and for teachers seeking to do something beneficial for them.

KINDERGARTEN COOPERATION: A CASE STUDY

In our first extensive analysis of the behavioral effects of cooperative games, we conducted an 18-week program with kindergarten children. Two classes were exposed to cooperative games and two other classes were exposed to traditional games. For the first eight weeks of the program (Phase I), the children had two 30- to 40-minute game sessions per week which were conducted by Jane McNally, a very capable graduate student. For the next ten weeks (Phase II), the teachers consented to teach the games themselves and the number of sessions per week doubled.

Rigorous behavior observations were taken by outside unbiased observers both before and after the games program. In addition, before the games began I asked the kindergarten teachers to jot down notes on anything that occurred during the program (in the gym or the classroom) which might reflect how the children were receiving the games. Some time after the program was finished, I conducted a cooperative games workshop with two of these teachers, Roberta Haley and Barb Champion, who together have over 30 years of teaching experience at the primary level. As they spoke to the workshop members sharing their perceptions about the games program, I was struck by something Roberta said. She talked about how I was running around trying to take all these fancy measurements, and about how she could clearly see what was happening "with her own eyeballs." It is precisely what she and others saw with their own eyeballs that I want to share with you now.

Roberta's first comments were recorded after her morning class had been playing cooperative games for three weeks, and continue from that point:

A group of eight children cleaning the paint center: They had organized themselves into groups of wet wipers and dry wipers and completed the task. Never have seen this before.

Bert calling David partner quite often and often seen with arms over each other's shoulders. Never noticed this before.

Children often asked is this the day for the games?

These games are real fun, is commented often.

Building a rocket, seven children wrapped paper around blocks, taped it, and colored pictures on it, with no fights. Amazing!

Fran comments on the "good games." She hasn't hit anyone for one week now. This used to be a daily occurrence. No one has tattled on any of her behavior for eight school days.

Three children playing "sticky popcorn" couldn't get undressed after recess—they were stuck together!

Twelve children walked down to gym stuck like popcorn, not my suggestion.

Sang "big ship" song spontaneously after they returned to class (note: song accompanies cooperative game).

Playing in the sand box, Bobby says to Marc, "Don't grab all the toys, we've got to share." They worked out the problem verbally!! Bobby has never been the verbal type, a good punch has generally been his solution.

When we have story time the children sit in a much smaller group (closer together). There appears to me to be much less, if any, complaining now about someone bothering another.

When I was teaching a dance, one that is done alone, children constantly got into pairs on their own.

One day in the library Fay said, "You gotta 'coperate.'"

Tina's comment to the Globe and Mail Reporter when asked which program (my gym or co-op games) she liked better was priceless. "I like them both equally as well but I prefer the co-op games." A perfect 5-year-old answer.

Barb Champion, who had one of her classes exposed to traditional games and the other exposed to cooperative games, also made some interesting observations and comments:

"Today was interesting. It was our first day in the gym since Phase I of the games program finished (end of first eight weeks). I had all the equipment out in five separate centers: large climbing apparatus, hoops, bean bags, tunnel, and balls. They were just there for use as each child saw fit, with no instructions. Each group of four or five children stayed at a center for four or five minutes and then moved on to another. This afternoon (cooperatives) the children reacted quite differently from the morning (traditionalists). They experimented with the bean bags carrying them head to head, shoulder to shoulder, etc. The hoop group connected themselves and made a long wiggly creature. Over at the ropes on the climbing equipment, children were taking turns helping another child get up and then pushing (swinging) him and taking turns. I was most happy with what was taking place and let them know enthusiastically. There is noticeably more cooperative play in the afternoon class.

Bonnie Brooks, a third kindergarten teacher, commented on her class, which was exposed only to traditional games. She noted that in her first free play session after the eight-week games program, "There was no cooperation in playing at all." All of the teachers involved in the program felt there was a definite increase in cooperative behavior in the co-op game classes compared to traditional game classes.

Barb Champion summed up her feelings about the program in the following way, "I felt the cooperative games were really ingenious and in most cases depended heavily on cooperation of two or more persons. The children really enjoyed the games. I think the children would cooperate even more if they were told that the game or activity would work better if they worked as a team and then in evaluation, the teachers or pupils could note that it went smoothly because everyone helped."

In my initial testing of cooperative games with kindergarten children, we did not verbally reinforce the cooperative game objectives. I wanted to see whether the games themselves would result in cooperative behavior. However the effect would probably be stronger if "good cooperation" was pointed out and reinforced. For example, by saying something like, "We couldn't have done that if all of you hadn't worked together," "Look how well so and so is cooperating," "You did it *because* you worked together," we would most likely breed more cooperation. This is an important point to keep in mind when attempting to get the best cooperative mileage out of the games, and something which we attempted to do in subsequent games programs.

Roberta Haley, who was particularly keen about implementing cooperative strategies, kept a detailed commentary on her observations for the second 2½ months of our program. The week immediately following Easter break from school Roberta noted, "Help, Terry!! My kids are so uncooperative this week—mean to each other, hitting, mouthy to each other, rotten at tidying up. Things have to look up!"

The next week she wrote:

"New week and better attitude in both kids and myself. We role played cooperation and noncooperation. They saw or seemed to see the errors of their ways last week. During role playing five out of seven groups choose cooperative scenes on their own. Many expressed "hate" for the noncooperative scenarios.

I am trying to incorporate cooperation using the center approach in the gym. It's working fine. At each of the five centers the children have a task to do using two or more in the group. Sometimes it may be only helping with a task like holding someone's feet for sit-ups.

Just came back from the gym. Do they ever put equipment away helping each other. We had everything imaginable out and it took only five minutes to clear. At this point I only point out what is left. They organize in groups by themselves to help each other.

Today Faye and Doug were cleaning up in class. Two of them were carrying one chair. "Mrs. Haley," yelled Faye, "Look at us. We're doing that thing you're always talking about, coopering!"

The most cooperation visible is at clean up time. It constantly amazes me how the majority (20 out of 24) team up and help each other. *There is no discrimination as to whether the mess is theirs or made by someone else.*

In direct contrast to this the teacher in the traditional games group noted, "A complete lack of cooperation in getting equipment out and putting it away. Most of my children will put one thing away and then simply line up or sit down, rather than help the next guy. They won't put things away that they didn't take out."

Toward the end of the co-op games program the children automatically tied the concepts of total participation and cooperation into singing games and other activities. For example on one occasion Roberta introduced a game called Elephants Walking on a Piece of String which the children had heard about on a record. For this game a piece of string is placed in a circle on the floor and the "elephants" balance while walking on the string. Everyone sings the following song:

Round and round on a piece of string
One (two, three, etc.) elephant is balancing
They thought it such a marvelous stunt
That they called for another little elephant

After each verse another elephant is added. "I had planned to go up to five elephants. When we reached five the children wanted to go up to 24 ('all of us'). We tediously (for me) did. When we were all balanced Mark decided we needed an ending to this game and suggested that I make up a song to say that we all fell down together inside the string.

Round and Round on a piece of string
24 elephants are balancing
They thought they'd like to be like a clown
So all of a sudden they all fell down.

They happily fell in a heap inside the string with squeals of joy and no rough stuff. Another point won for cooperation."

Roberta summed up her feelings the following way:

These children have learned so well to work in a group that sometimes a job that could be done by one person quickly turns into a five-minute group effort. For example, one day I said, "There are a few crayons out on that table." Christy said "I'll put them away." I looked over and there were five or six of them gathered around the table to help. So they emptied the entire large box holding eight small crayon boxes and started from scratch to put each little box in perfect order.

This kind of thing happens often, making me very aware that it is so necessary not only to teach cooperation but that it takes a lot of time to practice and learn how to do it. The common or more expedient way, from an adult point of view, would be to have said, "Christy will do it, the rest of you sit down." That kind of comment is so easy to make and so readily used. One has to change the entire attitude toward cooperation. It's not easy but is very possible and most rewarding.

Shortly before the end of the school year I briefly popped into two kindergarten classes which had been exposed to over four months of cooperative games. In one class, three youngsters were building a small log cabin together. A chain of passing was clear. One child passed a piece of wood to the next child and the next child passed it to the third who added it to the structure. "Here John, here Greg," accompanied their cooperative moments.

In another area two boys and a girl were building a large structure with large wooden blocks. They added levels to their tower together, often with two sets of hands placing a single block or with one child moving his block over so that the other child's block would fit.

In the open area of the room, two children began by riding together on a sturdy wooden truck and shortly thereafter took turns pushing one another on the truck. As I watched one child make a tinker toy by himself another lad whizzed by, screeched to a stop, said, "Hey Jim, that's real neat," and scooted off.

When I later walked into the other co-op games classroom I was greeted by the sight of six children carrying a big sheet of plywood with a bunch of objects on top of it. It was apparently a big table with some imaginary food on it. Naturally I was offered a piece and gratefully accepted. The quality of this imaginary food was surpassed only by the quality of cooperative social interaction within both of these classes.

The following week, some four-year-old children who would be attending kindergarten next year (rookies), joined in with the five-year-olds who were just completing their first year of kindergarten (veterans). There were approximately 20 veterans and 10 rookies in each classroom. No specific instructions were given to the children with respect to how they should behave.

In the co-op games class, two vets went over to a

sheepish looking rookie and asked, "Do you want to play in our sand box?"

No response.

"Do you want to paint?"

No response.

"Do you want to play at the family center?"

No response.

The rookie turned and walked away. The vets followed, persisting with their "Do you want to" questions. I wondered how long they would persist with their efforts. About five minutes later I noticed the three of them sitting on the floor working on a puzzle. I moved closer and saw the vets handing the rookie pieces of the puzzle, sometimes guiding his hand to where the pieces fit when he seemed perplexed.

I moved to another area of the room and found two more vets talking with a rookie. They asked a series of "Do you want to" questions to which he responded with a series of "No," "No," "No."

Kelly, one of the co-op vets, appearing momentarily exhausted, went over to the teacher and said, "These kids don't even know what they want to do." But she didn't give up yet.

She returned to ask, "Do you want to paint?"

"No!"

"We have lots of pretty colors. Do you like red?"

"Yes!"

"Come on, we've got lots of red."

Without delay, Kelly took him by the hand, put an

apron on him, took him to the paint center and handed him a brush. I think she wanted to move quickly to make sure he didn't change his mind. He proceeded to paint a picture in black and brown.

At one point a rookie was washing his hands in the drinking fountain. One of the female vets went over to him, took him to the sink and held the water on for him as he washed his hands, while a male vet got him a paper towel for drying and handed it to him. The female vet then unclipped his apron, took it off him, and hung it up.

In another instance a vet made a tower out of various sized blocks, and karate chopped it down as a rookie looked on admiringly. The vet asked the rookie if he wanted to try it. He nodded, to indicate yes. The vet then said, "Ok, I'll build one for you," which he proceeded to do. Later they built a structure together.

On still another occasion a veteran saw a rookie off in the corner by himself. He said, "I better be his friend, he doesn't got one." They played together for the remainder of the time.

In an adjoining non-co-op games class, there were very few cooperative events observed between veterans and rookies. Occasionally a veteran would take a rookie by the hand to show him something but the overall quality of cooperation was not comparable to the co-op class.

The difference between the classes was clearly expressed at a meeting with the teachers near the end of the school year: "Now my kids think of everyone being involved" (Co-op Class); "Mine don't do that at all" (Non-Co-op Class); "There's a definite difference in my classes. If there are not enough chairs, the children will share" (Co-op

Class); "If there are not enough chairs, they'll fight" (Non-Co-op Class).

On one occasion one of the outside observers had the unique opportunity of observing children from two different classes respond to a container of paint being spilt. The paint spilling was not an arranged event. It just happened spontaneously one day in both classes she was observing. The fact that one of these classes had been exposed to cooperative games and the other to traditional games was not known by the observer.

Her general comments about the manner in which the paint was cleaned up were interesting:

> "In the first class the children were more "together" in getting the job done. For instance one boy said "I'll squeeze the water and you wipe," and as the job was getting done he went over to the other side of the table and helped those children. One would squeeze and the other would wipe, another would get more water. Some comments made by the children while cleaning up included, "I will help you do this," "You do this and I'll do that," "Will you help me?" "We'll get this mess cleaned up."
>
> In the second class the cleaning was being done on a more individual basis. I did not notice many cooperative acts, such as those seen in the other class. It was as if each child had their own little section to clean. There was very little verbal or physical cooperation. In the first class the children were helping each other and got the task done quickly. Some of the kids in the second class kept blaming the person who made the mess and this group took longer to clean up the mess. I think I'd like the first group to clean my table!

The first group was a co-op games group, the second was a traditional games group.

During the last week of school after having seen me around for about six months, the co-op kindergarten children were asked why they thought I had been there.

They responded with, "I think he wants to play with us," "To talk to us," "To play games," "To help us play with each other and cooperate," "To learn us new games," "Cause he didn't have nothin better to do." They were all right, especially the last one.

Sometime after the games program had been completed, I asked the teachers if they would personally like to continue to run the games the following year. They were quite excited about continuing on with the cooperative games but wanted no part of the noncooperative games.

Barb Champion, who had observed one of her classes in each type of games program, put her reservation beautifully, "If you're really interested in better citizens, you can't have a control group."

It was obvious that she felt strongly that one of her classes would be missing something very important and that children at age five cannot afford to miss important human lessons. The other kindergarten teachers shared Barb's reservations.

Consequently all the kindergarten children in this school were exposed to cooperative games the following year, and every year since. Not only were the teachers sold on the concept behind the games but once they had seen some games in action, they began to make up new ones, adapt old ones, and come up with other good ideas to help cooperation become a more natural part of the children's lives.

ALTERNATE MEANS TO KINDERGARTEN COOPERATION

If our overall objective is to promote cooperation in kindergarten and preschool, we can obviously draw upon more than just cooperative games. We can involve the children in setting appropriate interpersonal behavior goals, through discussions on how they would like the other children to act toward them (e.g., to be friendly or mean). Specific, explicit examples can be drawn from the children with respect to general behaviors such as being friendly or nice. They can be asked how someone can be helpful, friendly or nice in different circumstances, for example at the sand box, painting center, reading center, etc. Concensus of desirable goals as perceived by the children can be recorded and posted in pictorial and block letters in the appropriate place, as a reminder for the children and the teacher. We are currently doing this in one kindergarten class and it is working well.

We can also take pictures or slides of children being helpful or cooperative, both in and out of games, and post the pictures around the room for the children to see. We can do this even if the shots had to be set up in the beginning. We can indicate that what we see in the pictures is what *we* agree that *we* like children to do in the classroom or gym.

We can talk about cooperation, about things that are possible because of cooperation, and set positive expectancies about cooperative behavior. Cooperative acts which occur during the course of the day can be pointed out to the class in an especially warm way by the teacher or peers.

From time to time the focus of *Show and Tell* can be to

show or tell how you helped or shared, or how someone else helped you or shared with you. In circle discussion the children can be asked for different ways to help or asked how many times they helped or shared today. Children can bring in, or paint, pictures of helping or sharing which can be shown to the class, talked about, and posted in the room. Posters, pictures and cartoons already in the room can be altered to show cooperative behavior or be replaced with new ones. The cooperative scenes depicted and values discussed could be related to play and games or any other aspect of a child's life.

Cooperative Imagery can be a useful step in sensitizing children to the possibility of cooperating. Young children have great imaginations and can be asked to imagine or visualize themselves helping in some cooperative scene which is presented by the teacher. This type of imagery can be done internally without actually having to act it out.

By using *cooperative role playing,* groups of two or more children can pretend to be something that requires everyone's help, or can act out situations about helping. For example, they can pretend that they *are* a string of beads, a forest, a caterpillar, a plane, a windmill, a bus or that they are *helping* paddle a big canoe together, build a log cabin, put up a tent, hold up a roof, push a car out of the snow, shovel snow off a rink, show a new student around, invite a shy person to join in their play, climb a mountain, or hold back a flood.

The children can think up helping scenes on their own, some of which are likely to come up in school, at home, on the street, or on the weekend while playing. They can also pretend that today they are the most helpful little person in the world and act it out. In some cases small groups can get together to decide on a very simple helping scene (in or out of games), work out a part for each group member, and act it out. The rest of the class can try to guess what is going on and why. Various kinds of skits and plays, along with music and dance, are rich with opportunity for cooperative learning.

Opportunities for peer teaching, cooperative game creation, and cooperative interdependent learning can be actively structured, guided and encouraged. Cooperative tasks such as those desired during clean-up time and when sharing equipment can be demonstrated and "cheered."

Videotapes of the children in class and in gym can be taken and desirable behavior can be clearly pointed out, discussed, and praised during the playback. In this way the children can serve as their own models of appropriate behavior. Exercises and songs can be done in a more cooperative fashion. Children's books and films can be produced which promote cooperation, and noncooperative ones, presently available, can be interpreted in a more cooperative fashion for the children. These are a few of the many ways to more cooperative games and cooperative lives.

Cooperative Games

For several years Pierre Provost, a former student and a good friend, has been putting cooperative principles into practice on a daily basis as an elementary school physical education teacher at St. Pius XII school in Hull, Quebec. While so many of us are talkers, Pierre is a front line doer. He has generated some excellent ideas on cooperative activities.

One day during the winter we had an exceptionally beautiful snowfall. There was lots of snow, the kind that really sticks. Pierre wanted to get his whole school out to make one giant snowball. The principal didn't exactly jump up and down over the idea but Pierre did manage to get a couple of classes out there working together. They rolled this little hunk of snow until it got so big that they could no longer move it. That was a cooperative effort which was highly visible and gratifying to all those involved.

Pierre has had great success with bringing together children from varied cultures (French, English, Portuguese) and different age groups, to play cooperatively. Over the lunch hour you will find sixth grade girls teaching jazz to students in fourth and fifth grades. You will also find some of the older children teaching and playing cooperative games with children in kindergarten, first, and second grades.

Pierre has tried a jigsaw puzzle route to learning and liking in his gym classes. He generally divides the class into groups of five with four or five different activity stations. Each person within each group is given one rule of the game for that station (part game method). Each has to contribute his or her rule for the game to be complete.

This idea for jigsawing in the gym grew out of Eliot Aronson's research with cooperative classroom learning. In his work students were placed in small groups with each person learning a unique portion of the material to be covered, teaching it to the rest of the group. Once the children realized that no one could do well without the aid of everyone else, and that each of them had a meaningful role to fulfill, they began to cooperate. This resulted in the children liking each other more, liking school more, feeling better about themselves (higher self esteem) and feeling happier. People at various age levels prefer cooperatively structured learning situations once they have become familiar with them.[1]

The first time I observed jigsawing in the gym was with a fourth grade class of 20 boys and girls. Once the five different components of a particular game had been handed out to five different individuals, they all got together at their game station to discuss their game. The group members usually spread themselves out on the floor in a close circle, talked for a short time, set up the equipment together, and began to play. The same procedure was followed at all four stations, each of which had a different game. When time came to rotate groups the children were asked to explain their game to the next group. The essentials of the new game were quickly relayed to the other group and everyone was again playing. This process continued until all teams had played all four games.

There was a tremendous sense of involvement in the gym, as is always the case when children create and play their own cooperative games. The children helped one another learn the game, set up the equipment together, and played the game together. Children were involved in the cooperative playing process all over the gym. They were moving, encouraging, cheering, and instructing. No one was left out, everyone was important, and it was obvious that they were enjoying themselves, without feeling rejected or useless. Pierre had to spend some time organizing the method but the children then took over entirely.

After the class I asked the children whether they liked teaching one another the games. All of their hands shot in the air. Every single one of them said they liked it.

This cooperative learning procedure can also be successful with much younger groups. For example, if kindergarten children had a few simple pictures of game components, they could show their fellow group members what to do.

In a second approach to jigsawing in the gym (whole game method), Pierre had one person in each group of five responsible for a total game. As the groups moved through the different stations, a different member of the group became responsible for introducing the new game. Although this was also successful it appeared that there was more cooperative interdependence in the first method, where each person had a portion of the game (part method).[2]

Pierre's students were exposed to many of our cooperative games while the games were being formulated. On one occasion he held a Cooperative Playday for his entire school. Thirty teams were made up of representatives from kindergarten and grades one through six. Besides participation, cooperation and enjoyment, a major objective of the playday was to have students learn the names of their schoolmates. On the information sheet distributed to teachers and students, Pierre stated, "I would like everybody in the school to know each other by name." Cooperation within and between teams, collective score games, and cooperative games with no losers were the rule of the day. Students explained the cooperative games to teachers and to fellow students. Points were awarded for participation and for cooperation, and bonus points were given for the number of fellow students group members knew by name.

Following his first year of trying to de-emphasize competition and aggression in the gym, while trying to promote cooperation and involvement, Pierre received letters from graduating sixth graders. The letters were written at the request of a sixth grade classroom teacher who asked her students to write letters to Pierre to express their thoughts on the gym program that year. I have selected a few of those letters to share with you:

> I like your way of playing games. We really only play to have fun. I never really enjoyed gym, only getting out of the classroom. But one reason why I didn't enjoy it was because everyone played to win. This year was different. We really participate in your games. I enjoyed gym very much and I know everyone else did too. Thank you very, very much.

> At the beginning of the year I thought you were a

very boring gym teacher. I thought about it and I realized that you were a very good gym teacher because you were helping us to help others and showing us how to play games without being so eager to win and to play without fighting. You were the first gym teacher that ever taught me gym like that. I really enjoyed gym this year.

Before you came to our school there was always competition everywhere. Your teaching has not only been good for me but I think it has been good for the whole school, including the teachers. I really had a good time in gym this year.

I have learned a lot this year and I owe it all to you. I learned a lot about participation and cooperation. I think your philosophy in gym is one of the best things anyone could learn. I also think if I ever become a teacher that is the method I would use. With thanks and gratitude.

I should point out that even after a year of exposure to cooperative games, all of the responses were not positive. Two of the 26 students in this sixth grade class wrote letters that expressed some reservations. One is presented below:

Thanks for a nice gym year. Even though I still think your method is to my dislike, I think that you have been a pretty good teacher. Sometimes I think that winning is the most important thing, like in hockey and baseball leagues, but in school I guess it's just to have fun. And thank you for teaching me that.

WHERE ARE ALL THE PIONEERS?

Besides our Ottawa-based team, I know very few people who are working on the development of cooperative games. There are probably many pioneers out there somewhere, but I am only aware of a few and I would like to share some of their ideas with you.

In 1975 CBS News filmed some of the cooperative games which we were in the process of developing. As a result of this program I received some very encouraging letters, mainly from concerned and supportive parents and teachers.

One letter came from Jack Coberly, a perceptual-motor teacher from South Bay School in Eureka, California, who was in the process of developing an activity program for his elementary school district. His program was based on success: "where children have a chance to succeed at every task given them." He pointed out the difficulty he was having in finding noncompetitive team activities and asked if I could forward any applicable activities. He closed his letter by saying, "It's good to know that I am no longer alone in seeing the lost look on faces of the majority of kids who are set aside to watch a few benefit from game and sport activities."

I was particularly pleased by the fact that Jack Coberly sent along some cooperative parachute and rope activities which he had found to be successful in elementary schools. In one such activity he attempted to introduce no loss, reversal or tie components into tug of war. To the sounds of music, verbal cues or silent gestures, players change sides during pull. They start switching from the beginning or end of the pulling line and change with a partner in the opposite position (numbers may be assigned). They attempt to see if a whole rotation can be completed before the game is over.

In a variation of this game, when a team is about to be dragged over the center line, the opposing team lets up pressure and gives the other team a chance to recover, or during the action, players continue to switch sides until teams are of equal strength. The objective is to pull as hard as you can to a standoff or tie.

Jim Deacove, from Perth, Ontario has come up with some really innovative cooperative games. He maintains that, "Games do not have to be games of conflict in which men are killing animals or cowboys are killing Indians or soldiers are killing soldiers. We try to provide games that involve positive values, attitudes of helping others."

One such game outlined by Jim and his associates is called Deacove Rounders. In this game each team tries to get its quota which is a score equal to the number of players on the team. A team stays up at bat until it gets its quota. If five players are on the team, it must get five runs in. When at bat, if you hit a grounder, you take one base. If you hit a fly ball and it's within the infield, then you take two bases, and if it goes into the outfield then you take three bases. However, the team in the field must catch the ball before a hit counts. For a grounder to count the ball must be fielded before it stops, for a fly, the ball must be caught. In this game the fielders are trying to get the ball not to put the other team out but to ensure that the "opposing" player gets on base. For one team to fill its quota it needs the help of the other team. For the fielding team to get up to bat they have to help the batting team fill its quota. When runners are on base they move ahead as their teammates get hits. Batters get three pitches but the pitcher has a reason to throw easy-to-hit pitches.

Parlor, or table games can also be re-worked to foster cooperation and the spirit of helping. Monopoly is not the only way to go, as has been clearly demonstrated by Deacove and his colleagues. They have devised, and are marketing through a mail order service[3], a series of different kinds of cooperative parlor games. Some of their games are still undergoing refinement but their focus is certainly admirable. Their game of Community reverses the emphasis found in the game of Monopoly. This game has common property, common resources, and common facilities. All players are playing together to build a viable community. Players must cooperate and help each other out and if they succeed in building the community they all win together.

In the game of Zen Blocks players work as a team trying to construct a three dimensional square. Each player has to use his share of the 14 blocks in a way that helps fellow players.

In the game Mountaineering, the players work as a team, confronting obstacles, as they ascend to the summit. The "climbers" share equipment and available resources. They plan their strategy and try to get to the summit and then to descend together safely to the chalet.

The basic approach to all of Deacove's games is completely different from other commercial parlor games. Other games involve a highly competitive principle. Simply stated, you must beat the other players to win. His games work the opposite way. They encourage the spirit of cooperation, the spirit of getting along with the other players. All players cooperate to solve the problems or obstacles the game itself raises.

"When we, as adults, were testing our games along with standard games, we began to learn how thoroughly conditioned we were to compete, how many resentful feelings creep in when playing the usual games, how pushy we could be, and it was a treat to play games that created the opportunity to help each other. It took a little unlearning at first, but it was worth it!" reported those who tested cooperative table games for Family Pastimes.

Ted Lentz, author of *Towards a Science of Peace*, was not only a front runner in the peace research movement back in the mid-fifties but was also a pioneer in the area of cooperative games. He and Ruth Cornelius came up with some interesting cooperative game structures and well designed cooperative games which are outlined in a manual entitled *ALL Together*.

In some of their games the underlying principle is for all players to finish simultaneously. For example, in Cooperative Chinese Checkers the goal is for all players to place their last marble into home place the same round. In Cooperative Checkers the normal rules are followed except that there is no jumping or moving backwards and the goal is for the two players "to change the black checkers and red checkers to opposite sides of the board at the same time." In their modified version of blanket toss, all players work together in an attempt to toss different sized balloons up into the air and back down through a hole which is cut into the center of the blanket.

Marta Harrison, members of the Friends Peace Committee, and other interested persons who contributed to the booklet *For the Fun of It* have come up with some excellent cooperative games. They believe, as do other pioneers in the area, that games can provide valuable opportunities for sharing and caring, for the development of trust and mutual support, for building a sense of community, if *everyone* feels included, participates equally, works together, and has a good time.

"The values we are hoping to build are ones of cooperation, caring, fun, a sense of group, and of respecting, helping and looking out for each other," says Harrison. By offering alternatives to competition and violence, they have found that people become more relaxed and open with each other and are better able to work as a unit. People are brought together through cooperation and laughter, and more human lines of communication are established. Musical Hugs is an example of a very simple and enjoyable cooperative game which can begin in nursery school. Children skip around the room to music and when the music stops everyone hugs another person. The music then starts up again and the process is repeated.

In Musical Laps a group of people form a circle, all facing in one direction, with hands on the waist of the person ahead. When the music starts, everyone begins to walk forward. When the music stops, everyone sits down very gently in the lap of the person behind them, to form a sitting circle. If the whole group succeeds in sitting in the laps without anyone falling on the floor, the group wins. If people fall down, gravity wins.

The New Games Foundation, based in San Francisco, is another pioneer group devoted to recapturing the fun of playing. They hold game tournaments to gain active support for their philosophy of play. In an interesting article entitled "The Games People Should Play," G. B. Leonard wrote about The First New Games Tournament held in California in 1973 and described some of the games which were created and played there.

In general a leisurely sense of informality prevailed, games were not played against time with pre-set intervals, players could wander in and out of the game, no specialized equipment was required, and team games were adaptable to groups of varying size.

One of the most popular games of the tournament was Infinity Volleyball. The normal rules of volleyball applied except that no specified number of players was required. As in regular volleyball one team could hit the ball no more than three times before sending it over the net. Players from both teams chanted aloud the number of times the ball had been volleyed and both teams shared the final score.

In another game, called Le Mans Tug-O-War, men, women and children lined up on either side of the bank of a creek, over which was stretched a huge rope. At the start signal everyone ran to the opposite bank, grabbed the rope and started pulling. "Children on the losing team have the most fun. They hold on to the rope and get a ride across the river from one bank to the other," reported Leonard. In this game, traditional winners and traditional losers both became "winners." The victors are pulling yet there are victories in being pulled.

Three years after the first New Games Tournament (many tournaments later), A. Fluegelman wrote a *New Games Book*. The book is essentially a collection of games created and played at these tournaments. Although there are some very good cooperative games presented in the book along with some excellent ideas for mass involvement, well over half the games outlined are clearly competitive in structure. Only about one quarter of the games are cooperative. Since no cooperative or competitive guidelines were provided for the game creation process, the relatively small proportion of cooperatively structured games is probably a reflection of heavy competitive conditioning and a limited range of cooperative game experience among most adult creators. This is a very good reason to rely more fully on the creative power of children for alternatives or at least to expose potential creators to alternative structures in order to broaden their creative scope.

Dan Davis, the director of recreation and gross motor development at the Benhaven School in New Haven, Connecticut, has been using cooperative activities for children with special problems. Benhaven is a school for multiply handicapped, brain damaged, and autistic children. The children who attend this school have language problems, perceptual problems, motor problems, and a host of behavior disorders. Many exhibit an almost total lack of normal interaction with their environment.

In an attempt to help deal with some of these problems, a series of dual balancing activities was designed to increase children's awareness of others and to promote cooperation. These activities have been useful in developing cooperation and awareness, even in extremely withdrawn autistic and brain damaged children. "Relatively high levels of cooperation and increased eye contact were established, which were exhibited in other school tasks such as moving equipment and materials from one place to another, as well as improvement in assembly line tasks performed in the prevocation workshop," reported Davis.

The cooperative activities utilized at Benhaven require the children to balance objects between them such as a tray with a block on it, as they move across a bench or walk across the floor.

These same procedures can be followed when going up and down stairs, while walking up and down hills, while going through an obstacle course, in snow, in water, on ice, etc.

We have played with some cooperative balancing ideas in Ottawa and have found that they are well received by "normal" elementary school children. We have had two children balance a bean bag on a hockey stick; balance a beach ball between two hockey sticks; hold a beach ball between their bodies without using hands, while walking across a line, bench or beam. In some cases we have had a series of bridges (benches) with a small space between one bench and the next. The children have to make sure they tell their partner when to step over the gap. We have also had youngsters go under benches and through hoops while still balancing the object, as a part of an obstacle course. The hoops add an additional cooperative challenge as the children must pick up the hoop and get through it or have another pair hold it for them while they go through, and then return the favor, which is what usually seemed to happen. We have also had two or more partners hold hands while walking in one direction on a beam and attempt to pass two or more partners walking in the other direction. To pull this off, awareness of others, physical contact with others, and cooperation within and between groups is essential.

As pointed out by Davis, "Awareness of others is increased in a situation where it would be impossible to function without this awareness. A form of cooperation is established, as well as the concept of working together with another person to achieve a common goal."

OTHER COOPERATIVE IDEAS

Almost any piece of equipment, situation or environment, can be structured or restructured for beneficial cooperation. Equipment can refer to both the cooperative use of equipment or the use of cooperative equipment. I will begin by mentioning a few things about the use of cooperative equipment. When 63 first and second grade children were in the gym, we rolled out numerous hoops, balls, scoops, and a dual balance board. The children were given five minutes of free play time. There was a striking difference between the behavior of the two children on the balance board and nearly all other children in the gym. These two children were linked together physically and balanced together for the entire time. Nearly all the others were active but in a totally independent way.

If something like a dual balance board or an old pair of water skiis with slots for three pairs of feet becomes available, you are almost assured that some cooperative interaction will occur. Similarly a swing built for two, a tricycle built for three, a rocking horse built for four, a slide built for five, a gigantic ball, a parachute, or a giant potato sack all seem to elicit cooperation among children. The equipment does not demand cooperation but certainly facilitates it.

A study by R. H. Quilitch and T. R. Risley demonstrated the importance of the structure of play materials on children's social behavior. When children were provided with "isolate" toys, social play occured only 16 percent of the time, whereas social play occurred 78 percent of the time when children were provided with "social toys."

In a similar vein, preschool activities which provide a prop for concurrent participation by two or more children, such as a teeter totter, elicit more than twice as much positive social interaction as do activities which provide for participation by one one child at a time, such as a tricycle.[4]

We have also found that certain types of equipment and materials tend to elicit cooperation. However, utilizing "isolate" toys under a new structure can also result in social play or cooperative play. For example beads, clay or trains may be viewed as isolate activities until children have learned to string beads together, to make collective clay castles, or link trains together. If children are requested to build one large tower wherein each has to contribute something, a cooperative social setting is created. It is the structure of the environment more than the structure of the material which influences a cooperative act, although both equipment and structures can be designed toward this end.

The cooperative use of noncooperative equipment can also have positive effects. One excellent, but often overlooked, opportunity to promote cooperation is in bringing equipment out and putting it away. Hoops, balls and sticks can be passed down the line from one person to the next. Larger equipment such as mats, beams and apparatus can be moved easily by small groups. When setting up an obstacle course, even preschool children are fully capable of carrying a large heavy bench when they all work together.

It is possible to come up with cooperative and enjoyable ways to move equipment. A team of children can all stand tall on their bench, jump off it, and even do sit ups while holding on to it (bench ups). Together they can quickly roll up a mat, run with it, sit on it, jump over it, and put it in the storage room. Partners can try putting balls away without using their hands or feet (e.g., using only their bodies).

Mutually beneficial interdependent goals are often available outside the games themselves. For example, if a group of individuals want to play a game on a rink which has snow on it, they can work together to shovel it off and then play. Similarly, such things as putting up rink boards, repairing a field, cutting ski trails, setting tracks, building shelters or log cabins provide an opportunity to bring individuals or teams together to work in unison for common mutually beneficial goals. It is also possible to bring groups together to build desired sports equipment, such as an outdoor obstacle course, a rope swing over water, a diving board, a rope bridge, nets, etc. This tends to promote friendly relations, to reduce conflict, and to provide something of concrete value.

Even within "individual" activities such as gymnastics there can be a great deal of helpful behavior if people spot each other, watch each others' moves, give constructive comments to one another, give one another encouragement. They do not have to be doing a dual routine for positive cooperative social interaction to occur.

Similarly in skiing or riding, techniques can be shared, the course can be checked out together, and the weekend can be enjoyed together in the outdoors.

In a study M. Bouet and I did in 1974, we found that experiences in the outdoors emerged as an ideal milieu for fun and cooperation. This environment seems to allow for new and exciting experiences together, for spontaneity and for sharing. It is also characterized by a sense of freedom from the constraints of organized competition, constant external evaluation and imposed human control. It has been found that children view the outdoors as a "place to have fun *with* friends."

Nature is a natural for cooperation because so many occasions for helping and sharing arise. This was reflected in the day-to-day living of some primitive cultures, some farming communities, and is also exemplified in certain present day outdoor sports, such as mountain climbing. Individual outdoor activities, such as cross country ski touring also provide many cooperative opportunities. For example, breaking a ski trail is very tiring for the lead skier, so naturally you tend to take turns in the lead.

Recently four of us skied out into the bush and a young man followed our newly broken trail. When he caught up to us he asked to take his turn breaking trail and later dropped back in line to catch his breath, as we all did. It was a very cold day and if you stood still for long you would begin to freeze. When we stopped for lunch we had to make a fire quickly to keep warm. Everyone did something to help, without being told. One person began to stomp down the snow for the fire area, two gathered firewood, and another got some things to sit on. The sooner we could all get our chores completed, the sooner we would all be warm and comfortable. We shared the warmth of *our* fire, we shared *our* food, we shared *our* thoughts. It was a fulfilling day, as are most days in the outdoors. We were all pleasantly exhausted by the time we returned home in the day. There was no competition, no score, no need to demonstrate that you were better than the next person, nothing done against another.

While nature provides numerous occasions for cooperation, it does not necessarily demand it. While it may be better for everyone concerned to cooperate in order to accomplish a task, some people may not recognize this. Initially, they may need to be guided along and shown that cooperation is, in fact, in their best interest. The outcome of the cooperative enterprise will generally reinforce their cooperative behavior.

When shooting rapids with two paddlers in a canoe, the need for cooperation is clear. If one fails to move his end of the canoe in the appropriate manner both end up bouncing off rocks in the water. You cannot overdo or underdo your contribution or the canoe will hit something, turn broadside and capsize. To complete a difficult run, you must not only know what you are doing, as well as what your partner is doing, but must also somehow communicate your intentions and adapt for one another. For a successful outcome and enjoyable experience, partners must work together.

After spending a month canoeing through some of Canada's most beautiful and untouched wilderness, six experienced Canadian canoeists independently wrote down what had been the highlight of the trip for them. Their peak experience was not the giant waterfalls, the turbulent white water, the flowing rivers, the sometimes tranquil, sometimes treacherous northern lakes, nor the animals, mountains and forests which they have come to love and respect. To a man, their peak experience was something very human which nature had allowed them to taste.

At one point in their trip they found in front of them a long lake. On its distant shore lay their destination for the night. They lashed their three canoes together, put up a sail, and rode with the wind. After a short time the wind ceased and the lake was calm. With their canoes still lashed together they began to paddle in unison into the sunset. Hours passed without a word being spoken, each man left to his own thoughts. A tremendous feeling of oneness and personal warmth was experienced silently by each member of the team. This was the highlight of two years of interdependent planning, weeks of each man pulling his own weight, being concerned about the safety of his fellow man, being tied to his paddling partner to maneuver through endless rapids, heavy winds, incredibly rugged portages.

The sharing and cooperation necessary to make this voyage successful can help us to understand the cooperative interdependence of some of our original people in years gone by.

---

[1]See Aronson (1975), Blaney, Johnson and Johnson, Haines, Lucker, and Blau in bibliography.

[2]See Appendix A for a specific example of "jigsaw" learning in the gym.

[3]For more information, contact Family Pastimes, RR #4, Perth, Ontario. K 7H 3C6

[4]See Doyle in bibliography.

Primitive People's Games

Although play and games greatly influence our way of acting, they have been largely ignored in terms of potential impact on socialization. We have been content to let games be, without much concern for the vital role they play in shaping children's values and behavior. After all, "They are only games . . . mere child's play!" The social significance of children's play and games continues to be overlooked in contemporary societies as it was when anthropologists first began to study more "primitive" cultures. Let's have a closer look at some primitive people's play.

Sowada, who for many years lived among the Asmat of New Guinea, was the first outsider to settle in the twin villages of Saowa and Erma. He reported that the Asmat shared what they had with a visitor. They considered it an insult to send a person away empty-handed and would call any selfish person, "Mban doso ipir," a man with a putrid hand.

"How rude we Westerners must have seemed when we arrived with all sorts of goods yet did not divide them among the people. A man, if he possesses, shares; but he also realizes that at some time or other he will receive something in return," wrote Sowada. He was one of the few people to talk about the introduction of competitive games in a primitive culture:

When we taught the school children to play soccer, the game invariably ended in a tie. Only after much prompting did the children learn to play to win the game. The spirit of competition soon began to infringe upon other aspects of Asmat culture. Every year the men of Erma built new dugouts, and each clan entered one of its canoes in a race. With gusto the expert rowers paddled their dugout across the river, but they reached the opposite bank at almost the same instant. During one annual race, however, a dugout arrived two lengths ahead of the others. Such great consternation resulted among the people that they did not hold that event again.

The mountain Arapesh of New Guinea is a society characterized by active helpfulness, a high value being placed on the needs of others. The devotion of the entire people is to a common nonmaterial ideal. The Arapesh ideal man is one who demonstrates an all-around devotion to community ends and one who is hospitable, gentle and understanding.

In this cooperative culture small children are given a great amount of affection by everyone and come to see adults as kind and loving. Children are repeatedly taught that they must not hurt others and fighting between children is not permitted. Emphasis is placed upon responsiveness to the requests of others.

During social functions children are seldom separated as a group from adults. For example, where there is a dance or feast, women dance with small children on their shoulders.

The games which children play are simple and non-competitive. Margaret Mead reported two specific games of Arapesh children, both of which could be classified as cooperative games with no losers. In one game all the children squat, hold on to the waist of the child in front of them, and pretend to be one big snake. In another game involving cooperative role playing (called Cutting the Sago Palm), one child (the palm tree) is carried in the arms of the others.

It is interesting to note that when competitive football was introduced from the outside in the 1930's, small boys began playing enthusiastically with a lime fruit. However the game resulted in frequent tears, agitated outbursts, and finally in refusals to play. I assume this occurred as a result of a rejection of the basic structure of the game or as a result of the little boys being conditioned to perceive the outcome as increasingly important. However Mead only made fleeting reference to this incident as is often the case when anthropologists refer to play and games.

The Tangu people of New Guinea play a popular game known as Taketak, which involves throwing a spinning top into massed lots of stakes driven into the ground. There are two teams and players on each team begin by trying to touch as many stakes as possible with their tops. In the end the players play to tie, not to win. This requires great skill as players must sometimes throw their tops into the midst of many stakes without touching a single one. The game goes on until an exact draw is reached or until there is mutual recognition of parity. Taketak expresses a prime value in the Tangu culture, that of moral equivalency, which is also reflected in the equal sharing of foodstuffs among the people.

The games and stories of the highly cooperative Bathonga society of South Africa also reflected a closely integrated, easy going, frictionless pattern of life. There was a great deal of comradeship in their games and, as was probably the case in many primitive cultures, games occupied a good part of their time.

In speaking about the Australian Aboriginal people of the Western Desert (Pitjantjatjara), R. Tonkinson wrote, "Contrary to earlier assertions about hunting and gathering peoples, we now know that the task of obtaining daily food rarely occupied more than a few hours of the Aborigines' time. . . . Their leisure hours were many, whatever the season, and the opportunities to be sociable were endless." Leisure activities such as games, sand drawing, and storytelling played an important role in the transmission of Pitjantjatjara culture, which is still dominantly oriented toward amicability, sharing, kinship, solidarity, and peace. Throughout their literature the themes of cooperation and adult love for children recur again and again.

One of the few people who has had the opportunity to immerse himself in Aboriginal play and games is Ian Robertson from the Salisbury College of Advanced Education in South Australia. I have talked at length with Robertson about his work with the Pitjantjatjara people of South Australia. I viewed his films on the Musgrave Ranges with great interest and saw many parallels to cooperative cultures that I have personally studied.

"To the eyes of an Aboriginal child the environment

is ideal with trees, sand-dunes and rock outcrops to climb, rockpools to swim in, limitless flat areas on which to run and roam unbounded, small animals to chase and catch, many playmates and few restrictions imposed by parents in this rich environment. Childhood is a time of happiness," according to Robertson.

In one game children play, called Spear the Disc, the players form into two groups and take up positions about 15 yards apart. As a bark disc is rolled back and forth between them, each group in turn tries to spear the target as it passes.

As C.P. Mountford reported:

> There did not seem to be any spirit of competition, either between the boys themselves or the groups; their enjoyment was gained from the success of spearing the bark disc. . . . It was while photographing from a jutting rock, some 30 feet above the players, that I noticed the picturesqueness of the scene below. . . . In the middle of the scene, like actors on a stage, were 20 or more naked brown-skinned children, their bodies almost luminous in that brilliant light; some poised like bronze statues as they waited, tense and eager to spear the oncoming disc; others running, jumping and laughing from sheer joy and the excitement of the game.

Traditional Canadian Inuit play a very similar game where members of one group roll hoops, one after the other, past members of another group so that they can attempt to throw spears through them. The groups then reverse roles.

In a Master's thesis on traditional Australian Aboriginal games, Mike Salter concluded that: 1) the games were played for their enjoyment, and victory was of very minor importance; 2) games rules were minimal and many of the activities were of a group nature; and 3) there was maximal participation in play and games and these activities were used to solidify internal relationships and promote positive social interaction and goodwill.

Robertson describes a typical game of Australian Rules Football he observed in 1974 as follows:

> As each team filed onto the oval, players and spectators from the other group clapped their appreciation in a most courteous manner. After the teams ran onto the oval they formed a semi-circle about the center of the oval. The first priority of this large circular gathering of men was to ensure that each side had an equal number of players, with no particular concern for the usual number of eighteen players. After a count by the captains it became apparent that Ernabella had one more player than Amata. A chorus of "one more" resulted in an unsuspecting individual being coopted from the small crowd of onlookers. This first concern for equality and fairness was a theme that became more evident as the match progressed. Although two players (opponents) may occasionally contest the ball, most men appeared to enjoy each other's company and were continuously engaged in conversation. Bumping and tackling one's opponent is very rare although spectacular falls are appreciated by all.

In addition, the games are not time bound. They may be quickly terminated or in some instances may last from midday to sunset. In the eight matches that Roberston had seen, all had been played with "the highest degree of sportsmanship, and with complete adherence to the few essential rules."

The need for umpires in this setting is in direct contrast to the football games played in Australian cities, where I might add they are experiencing the same problems with youth sports that we are facing in North America. But because the concepts of fairness and equality are already present in the Aboriginal situation, it need not be imposed by an impartial authority dressed in white.

It is interesting that when competing as individuals Aboriginal school children want to excel only if it is directed toward the benefit of the group. To distinguish yourself from your peers for your own selfish ends is considered quite unethical. "Frequently in running races children would deliberately slow down in order to cross the line with a friend," reported Robertson. By contrast relay races are run in full earnest as they are probably perceived as a cooperative form of competition. When the adults ran their races Robertson had the feeling that they were running for their "mob" and not for themselves.

Softball is now a popular game among Aboriginal women. The importance of fairness in games and life was again revealed here when one teacher failed to persuade the runners to steal bases. "The idea of running before the ball was pitched, and hit, was quite unacceptable to the girls," reported Robertson.

Soccer was played for the first time by the Aboriginal girls at Ernabella while Robertson was there. Only two rules were used: 1) you cannot use your hands; and 2) this mob goes this way and that mob goes that way. The game was an immediate success.

Similar success was apparent with "rule free" games played among traditional Canadian Inuit.

When old Eskimo people in the western artic were asked whether there had been a code of sportsmanship in such games, "although most did not understand the concept of sportsmanship, several commented that if a player used unnecessary roughness the older men would see to it that this behavior was terminated," said Gerry Glassford, a friend and respected colleague from the University of Alberta, who first introduced me to the Canadian arctic. He did an extensive review of traditional Canadian Eskimo games. He was also instrumental in the revitalization of Eskimo games in the north after their demise. Many of the Inuit games and forms of amusement discussed by Glassford fall under my classification of cooperative games with no losers. Others could be categorized as semi-cooperative games, collective end games, or reversal games. Barring rare exceptions, I think it is safe to say that our original people participated in game-like activities in a cooperative, friendly and harmonious manner.

One reversal game which was a favorite among Eskimo groups was called Nuglutang. A small spindle-shaped piece of antler with a hole in it was hung from the roof. The players stood around the target with a sharp rod in their hand. Each person attempted to drive the tip of his rod into the hole in the target, all at the same time. The first player to place his rod in the target was the first winner and he put up, as a stake, anything he wished that had value. The second winner assumed ownership of the first stake, but in turn replaced it with another. Thus, in our terms, the only one to lose anything was the first winner, and the only one to win anything was the last winner. Many excess goods (knives, cartridges, etc.) were exchanged in this manner. I watched one group of Eskimos playing this game with a great deal of joviality and laughter. The last player to put his rod into the hole had great difficulty primarily due to the extent of his laughter and the movement of the spindle. The fact that he was the last to accomplish the feat seemed to have no bearing on his own enjoyment or the enjoyment of those around him.

A dart game with a similar orientation was played by the Inuit during the months of darkness. A dart was thrown at a small piece of caribou fat in the middle of the floor. One player would set up a prize and another would aim for the target. The winner, the one who hit the target, was in turn expected to put up a prize for the next contestant. As with the previous game the only real winner in white man's terms was the person last to win, as he did not have to replace the prize. These games are among the few reversal games I have been able to document in primitive cultures, with the exception of reversal hide and seek.

One form of hide and seek called Erigak, played by Eskimo children, was the complete reverse of that played among Euro-North American children. The Eskimo children came together in a closely packed circle facing inward and downward so that they could not see. One child hid and the others then sought him out. When discovered, he was chased by the group. The first player to touch him, an act labelled the "FIRST HARPOON" would then hide. Thus the game continued.

Robertson, in reporting a similar orientation among the Aboriginal people of South Australia, said, "Frequently, by comparison to Western culture, the role of the group and the individual are reversed in games like hide and seek. In our culture, the seeker goes looking for the group. However, it is the group members that cooperate in looking for one or two individuals 'lost' in the bush. It does not take much to extend this concept to a comparison of our two cultures. The Aboriginal culture stresses cooperation and group solidarity, and our Western culture emphasizes competition and individual attainment."

F. Boas described a cooperative game played by the Caribou Eskimo in the 1800's. The game was called Igalukitaqtung and had both cooperative means and cooperative ends. The object of the game was to keep a sealskin ball in motion without it touching the ground. This was probably a forerunner to collective score volleyball. Cooperative activities with no losers, such as drum dancing (Aghi) and blanket toss (Nalukatuk), were favorite leisure activities of the traditional Eskimo. The blanket toss required the cooperative effort of a large group of 15 to 30 players who stationed themselves around the outside edge of a large walrus hide blanket, approximately 10- to 15-feet wide. One person would stand in the center of the blanket. By collectively pulling sharply outwards and upwards, the outside players would catapult the center person high into the air. According to Eskimos interviewed by Glassford, the game was played for the sheer thrill of the experience.

Mukpaun is an example of a semi-cooperative game which used to be played by Eskimos of all ages and both sexes. It is a baseball type game played with one base, and each player is permitted to have a turn at bat before the two sides exchange roles. No score is kept.

There are many additional examples of traditional Inuit activities. The common thread running through all of them is the fact that the games were found to be dominated by few-step operations and low structural organization. The division of labor within any game was of the lowest level, and player specialization was unknown. Most of the traditional games had minimal requirements in terms of space, equipment, organization, and preparation. They were characterized by simplicity, spontaneity and involvement. Many of the activities involved all the nuclear family and involvement reached a peak during the winter months when hunters could spend more time at home.

The motive to beat or conquer others was not apparent. The motive to be self reliant, strong, helpful, to share and to have fun was very apparent. The surpassing of natural or imposed obstacles appeared to be more acceptable and more challenging than attempts to top or topple other men. "Losing" games did not involve losing face.

This, of course, was before the real onslaught of the Euro-North America influence. Since that time, age segregation, sex segregation, division of players and people into winners and losers, and extrinsic rewards have become more prevalent in many activities. When searching for quality in games and lives, it appears that we must look back to look forward.

NORTHERN GAMES REKINDLED

In 1970, Inuvik, Northwest Territories, (the place of man) hosted the first annual Northern Games in modern times. Northern Games was conceived with the idea of bringing together northern people in friendly competition and cooperation, with emphasis being placed on traditional skills, games and dancing of Indian and Eskimo people. It was thought of as a festival in keeping with the traditional gatherings of northern peoples of years gone by. It was hoped that cooperation and sharing would once again play an important part in the events.

According to the Games organizers, nonnative sports-minded people often do not understand the idea behind the Northern Games, as they are used to thinking in terms of regimented athletic contests where winning appears to be the dominant aim. Northern Games are oriented another way. Sharing the fun and learning from each other is part of the theme. Emphasis is on playing rather than upon watching other people play. The competitive aspect is not the be-all and end-all. No one goes home dejected because they have not won an event. "Northern Games is people. Northern Games is friendly sharing. Northern Games is fun," they proclaim.

When it gets down to the nitty gritty of the events, they customarily take place according to "northern time," which means whenever people feel the time is right. In the Good Woman Contest, women from many settlements demonstrate their skills in sewing, cooking, preparing food and skins, and dancing. Traditionally, looks were not the prime asset of a good woman. A "good woman" needed to know how to sew well, to take care of a family, to be good in the skills of fire lighting, tea boiling, fish cutting, animal skinning, and to be well coordinated. It is for this reason that these skills are a part of the Good Woman Contest.

At the 1976 Northern Games in Coppermine, Northwest Territories, I observed many signs of a healthy traditional orientation toward activities, particularly among the older participants. The spirit of the past was rekindled, at least for the duration of the Games.

A great deal of time was devoted to drum dancing which was clearly noncompetitive in nature. Each dance began with several of the old men beating out a rhythm and concluded with almost everyone in sight participating, including young children strapped to their mothers back or in the arms of their brothers and sisters. The dancing continued through the sunlit night and into the wee hours of the morning.

The clearly cooperative Blanket Toss was among the favorite activities. After the adults had completed a tossing session, the children spontaneously rushed to the blanket, took hold of it, and tossed one another. Instead of the normal cries of "my turn, my turn," to which we are so accustomed on the outside, I witnessed the opposite. Young children called out the names of their friends, "your turn, your turn." Constant was the warmth of laughter and giggling among the tossers and tossees.

Probably the greatest amount of harmony, sharing and sheer fun was evident in the Good Woman events. In the Tea Boiling Contest, a group of approximately eight middle-aged women of all shapes and sizes lined up awaiting the signal to start. It was over and above their talking, giggling and laughing that the starter bellowed "go!" They ran, leaped and waddled to a wood pile and began clutching at the wood, amid roars of laughter. The fires were quickly ignited for the most part (no paper please) and the pots of tea were soon simmering on the fire. When one woman had trouble getting her fire going, another contestant offered her some wood while uttering, "What's wrong with your fire?" "I dunno!" Another woman, who was having difficulty getting her fire hot enough, laughed heartily while repeating, "Just about boiled!" The woman who finished first started to dance while other contestants stopped to joke with her. As each of the remaining women lifted her simmering tea from the fire she offered it to everyone around, sometimes emptying her pot before getting to the locally recruited "judges." It was more important to the women to share their tea and have people enjoy it than to have it judged and declared the best.

The Bannock (Bread) Making Contest, over open fires, was similar to Tea Boiling in terms of harmony, enjoyment and sharing. The cooperative orientation toward the event was clearly depicted when, *during the contest*, the bannock makers were confronted with frozen bars of lard. Two women competitors helped each other cut the lard, which each needed for her bannock. The clean up after each session was also very cooperative with all the women picking up, chatting and laughing as they washed up afterwards. One participant was asked if it was important to make the bannock fastest. She replied, "It's not important to be fastest, it's important to make good bannock."

In the Seal Skinning and Fish Cutting contests the women sometimes exchanged or shared cutting implements. On one occasion, "in the heat of the competition," one woman said, "So dull." Her competitor responded, "Try this." A knife was exchanged for an ulu (Inuit cutting blade).

The events at the Northern Games which most closely resembled competition on the outside were engaged in by the young men. In one such event, called the One Foot High Kick, contestants attempted to kick a ball suspended in the air and land on the same foot with which they kicked. The ball was raised after everyone had either kicked the ball, or had made several attempts. The atmosphere surrounding this competitively structured event resembled what I have experienced during gymnastic exhibitions, as opposed to competitions. Each young man made an earnest attempt to do a good kick but the world did not end with a miss. During the event the participants joked with one another, gave each other constructive suggestions, and applauded one another. If a contestant missed, he was afforded a few more tries, sometimes after a little rest or after a few tips from a judge or from a fellow competitor. In some cases the contest continued until the last kicker could go no higher, while in other cases they stopped when three or four were at a particular height, which is more in line with the old days. Contestants generally smiled after their kick whether it was successful or not. In the final high kick event, when only two competitors were left, they continued to smile, to chat with one another, and to clap for one another after each jump. On only one occasion over the course of the games did anyone show overt signs of frustration or dejection after a "loss." In this case, after missing a kick at a particular height a young man walked over to the ball and wacked it with his hand. As the frame holding the ball rocked back and forth some bewildered looks overtook the smiles on the old people's faces. Men of all ages took part in tests of strength where the winner continues to take on challengers, one after another. What this does, in effect, is to equalize a very powerful contestant so that eventually someone over-powers him. It may be the 15th challenger who is actually weaker, but at the moment, much fresher. While members of the older generations noted that jerking or twisting was not permitted in these events, some of the younger Eskimos felt that tricks could be used.

The fact that some traditional "ways of winning" were still in effect became more evident toward the end of the games. In most events people did not know who had "won" and no one seemed to care. There was, however, an informal awards ceremony held as the 1976 Games came to a close. Although a few plane loads of people had already departed, others joined in to share the victories. Laughter, clapping and cheering were evident for all victors.

When one woman was declared the winner of the Traditional Dress contest, two of her competitors seemed to be overwhelmed by her victory. They were so excited that they beamed with delight and embraced her affectionately. The fact that they were also in the contest seemed to have no bearing on their happiness for her.

When a tie was announced between two men in an event which required balancing on one hand and reaching as high as possible with the other (The One Hand Reach), one man quickly decided that the other should get the award "because he is quite a bit shorter."

As I reflect back on the 1976 Northern Games, it is apparent that one of the greatest occasions for cooperation occurred the week before the games. Forty-two tents had to be set up to house the participants; food, which was later cooked by the participants themselves, had to be divided into boxes for each tent; dried meat and fish had to be cut into chunks; seals had to be hunted; signs had to be made; out-houses, complete with "honey buckets," had to be con-structed, etc.

Men, women and children helped set up the tent village which took several evenings of hard work. I was particularly impressed by a small group of young females who volunteered their time, day after day, doing whatever needed to be done, both before and during the games. Small children helped carry large pails of muktuk (whale blubber), young women cut dried whale meat, hunters brought in seal and caribou.

As the excitement of the upcoming games was building among the children, I chatted with a young Eskimo boy. I mentioned that lots of people would be arriving tomorrow, for the games. Alert and wide-eyed, he asked, "Are there going to be Indians?" I nodded, yes. His eyes grew wider as he splurted out, "Cowboys, too?"

The whole atmosphere surrounding the games was one of genuine warmth and togetherness. Participation was open to all. Participants actually outnumbered spectators. Since acceptance as a worthy person was not dependent upon placing in an event, people were free to enjoy themselves and each other. The weight of the world was not on any contestants' shoulders, nor were any international heroes created. It was just a group of people getting together to play, to share a part of their culture, to share a part of themselves, and to have a good time.

Cooperatively oriented people in many cultures, including our own, can bring a special kind of orientation to a game that makes it constructive rather than destructive. Likewise, cooperatively oriented play and games can bring a special orientation to people, which frees them to be more human. They can work, play, enjoy, improve . . . but at no time have to put down someone else. Clearly they control the competition, it does not control them—in games and life.

Cooperative Closing

If you've read this far you undoubtedly realize that I am concerned about the direction in which our society is moving and feel that we have a responsibility to socialize people so that they behave in a more humane way. I have discussed the cooperative social environment from which man has come, the destructiveness which has come to exist, the sparks of human compassion which remain, and the human warmth which we still have the potential to develop. I have tried to present a rationale for cooperation, a basic framework which promotes cooperation, and some cooperative alternatives. All of these cooperative strategies are aimed at preparing people to be "fittest" for *meaningful* human survival and *mutually beneficial* coexistence.

Bertrand Russell was looking ahead with considerable foresight when he wrote, "Competition considered as the main thing in life is too grim, too tenacious, too much a matter of taut muscles and intent will, to make a possible basis of life for more than one or two generations at most. After that length of time it must produce nervous fatigue, various phenomena of escape, a pursuit of pleasure as tense and as difficult as work (since relaxing has become impossible) and in the end the disappearance of the stock."

During a Canadian speaking tour in the 1970's, Margaret Mead made the point very strongly that the future quality of human life, as well as the survival of the human species, will be dependent upon cooperative behavior along with a concern and respect for the rights of others. This mutual concern will have to extend beyond borders and beyond generations, to include those who will inhabit the earth several generations hence. Leaders in many fields support this position.

In Ashley Montagu's words, "The more cooperative the group, the greater is the fitness for survival which extends to all its members." In Abraham Maslow's terms, "We must understand love; we must be able to teach it, to create it, to predict it, or else the world is lost to hostility and suspicion."

As expressed by Pierre Trudeau at the 1976 Habitat Conference, "The only path open to us is to move toward a common passion, a conspiracy of love." As suggested by Mother Teresa at the same conference, this conspiracy begins with each and every one of us, by turning our words of love and sharing into action.

It's frightening to look at the events of today and contemplate what tomorrow holds in store. Yet all of the major problems confronting man, including violence, destructiveness, war, poverty, pollution, crime, corruption, human exploitation, even rampant strikes and inflation, can be solved by a new ethic—a cooperative ethic.

Cooperation breeds new motives, new attitudes, new values and capabilities. If our future quality of life, and perhaps even our survival, depends upon cooperation, then unless we are fit to cooperate, to help one another, to be open and honest with one another, to be concerned with one another, to be concerned with future generations, we will perish. Consequently, if we are really interested in survival and a higher quality of life in the future, we will move away from a stress on ruthless competition against others and begin to emphasize cooperation with and a concern for others, both in and out of games.

Unless we change our destructive course each of us will eventually be the target of our own barbarianism. We must abandon this madness, in which something is not expected to be profitable materially or politically, so it is rejected no matter how profitable it may be to humanity. We must put an end to placing so much emphasis on money, power, or a score in a game, that the value of people is destroyed in the process.

Games and sports are reflections of the society in which we live but also serve to create that which is reflected. Many important values and ways of behaving are learned through play, games and sport. Games are important, primarily because the target population is children in the process of developing, who spend countless hours engaged in game-like activities. In our games we must think of the kind of society which we would like to have and reward children for behavior which would be desirable in that society. One of the greatest lessons to be learned from our cooperative experience is that we can create or alter games to accomplish specific humanistic objectives.

Yet, this is only one medium of change. There are many others. Take a moment and think. How can you readjust your games so that helping, sharing, consideration, and mutual trust are encouraged? How can you change the values in your life to ensure that people come out on top? Do you have occasions where people come together to work for common mutually beneficial ends at home, at work, at school, during your free time? Do you utilize the opportunities which do exist?

What about your family? Do parents and children actively do things together where they are equally important contributors, or is there a great deal of age segregation so that members of the same family take part in the same activity, at the same time, but in different places? Do you see adults playing with children, older children playing with younger ones or is there very little cooperative personal contact among all ages?

When I look back on my own upbringing, I feel fortunate to have had so much cooperation and trust among my family members. We did many physically active things together. For example, as a spin off of my father's days in the circus, we had a family act (pyramids and acrobatics) which required total cooperative interdependence among all six family members. It was a situation involving cooperative means and cooperative ends, with no competition and no age or sex segregation. This was one of the many interdependent situations that brought my family so close together.

It was this kind of interdependence toward other ends that brought primitive people and extended families of the past close together. Everyone had some important interrelated role to play, even the children. People cooperated, all contributing to common good. The lack of these experiences contributes to pulling present-day people apart.

At one time it was not necessary to create conditions for cooperation and interdependence, as they existed naturally and still do in certain cultures. However, in mainline North America we have "progressed" beyond cooperation, as the result of a runaway competitive and materialistic ethic. The reason people in some cultures, particularly the children, seem so happy, so friendly, so self assured, so sincere, relates to their cooperative life style.

When people blossom among genuine cooperation, they grow to like one another, to appreciate one another, to share with one another, and to know that each has a meaningful role to play. This sincere concern for one's fellow man, which grows out of cooperative ventures, is essential to a high quality of life. Many great people have expressed this feeling, particularly as they approach the ends of their lives. Yet the peoples of the world have not yet heeded their advice.

Perhaps this goal seems too distant . . . too remote. But we can change the orientation of our own lives and the orientation of our own games. We can in fact be more influential in changing these two areas than anyone else. Yes, we can do something. We can effect positive change, or at least neutralize the rising tide of negative change. Furthermore, if games which in the past have been viewed as necessarily competitive can be re-structured to foster cooperation, then certainly other aspects of our society can be altered. If people are willing to act, in time, even the most exploitative organizations could begin to subscribe to our new ethic.

Perhaps we cannot hope to affect the deeply prejudiced person. He already knows his own reality and doesn't want to be confused by facts. As Aronson said, deeply prejudiced people are virtually immune to information. But I think we have some legitimate hope of changing the mildly prejudiced people. And we must also provide support for those who are already working toward cooperative lives.

Although we may never reach all our humanistic ideals, if we do not have ideals to reach for, we will certainly never begin to move toward them. To merely resign oneself and say, "That's the way it is, that's the way people are, everyone does it, there's nothing we can do about it," is to be mistaken and will allow future generations to suffer for our misdirections. What is, today, does not necessarily have to be, tomorrow.

I have great confidence in the youth of any culture who have been nurtured under cooperative wisdom, combined with an element of humanism. If the children raised within this environment can hang on to their humanistic values, until they become adults, the parents, the teachers, the leaders, then the values themselves will be assured some element of permanence, in games and in life.

Whether we speak of mini-societies called cooperative games or of societies as a whole we are faced with similar kinds of problems. Cooperative children are often exposed to noncooperative adults and noncooperative adult structures before they have had a chance to grow into fully functioning adults themselves. This will be one of the most difficult problems to overcome.

At this point, we can only plant the cooperative seed, we may never personally witness humanity in full bloom. However, it is conceivable that an entirely new ethic could permeate society within one or two generations *if* cooperation were actively promoted at different age levels and in different environments. By the time today's preschool children have children of their own, the foundation for a more humanistic society could be solidly implanted. What we desperately need now are people committed to solutions and to the implementation of solutions. The quality of our games and lives hang in the balance.

"You're a dreamer," some will say, "an idealist." I am reminded of something I once heard: When a man dreams alone, it is only a dream; when many dream together, it is the beginning of a new reality. Perhaps we need more "dreamers" whose visions of today allow them to glimpse a better tomorrow.

As I search for final words with which to close this book I am left with the feeling that alone I am nothing, my ideals are empty. The strength of my thoughts lies in their capacity to free others to dream and to act.

So I'm back where I started at the beginning asking myself, why bother? Did I waste my time putting all these thoughts down, was it merely an academic exercise, will it ever make any difference?

The power of dreams, of ideals, of change, rests within people, everyday people . . . like you and me.

Appendix

JIGSAWING IN THE GYM WITH COOPERATIVE GAMES[1]

COOPERATIVE GAMES TEACHING BY PEERS—PART OF GAME METHOD

Four or five stations, five persons in a group. Each person has the knowledge of *one part* of a game. The partial explanations of the games are handed out for a few minutes before each game. One unique piece of information goes to each team member. The team members then get together and share their knowledge so they are able to learn about the different components of the game and then play it.

Sample Game Instructions, for Balloon Goodminton from Canada, follow. Remember that each player is told about only one part of the game:

Part 1: Equipment: Use a regular badminton net that is attached to two poles, five racquets, and a balloon. The small racquets will be used for this game. Set up the equipment together.

Part 2: Rules of the Game: One player starts by hitting the balloon and then each player on that side must get a pass before the balloon is hit over the net. The objective is to make as many passes as possible over the net without having the balloon touch the ground.

Part 3: Scoring: Count the number of passes over the net out loud. You stop counting and start over again when: the balloon touches the floor; a player touches the net; the balloon is broken; two racquets touch each other; a racquet goes over the net. Each time you start over, a new person serves.

Part 4: Keep Up Technique: Try to keep the balloon way up in the air so your friend has a chance to get it. Use an underhand motion to serve. To hit the balloon over the net try an overhand, a side arm, and backhand motion. Remember the balloon should be hit and not carried around on your racquet.

Part 5: Playing Strategy: Three people are on one side and two are on the other side. With two on one side you can play one up and one back. In this case the person closest to the net has to take care of the front part of the court and the back person takes care of the back part of the court. You can also play side by side, each being responsible for half of the court. How could this last strategy be used for the people with three on a side?

The amount and type of information provided is dependent upon the specific game and the age group. We have found this jigsaw method successful in teaching new cooperative games and unknown games from different cultures (e.g. Rounders from England, Gorodki from

Russia). For known games (e.g. Canadian Lacrosse) we provided a short history, different methods of play (box and field lacrosse) and a little more precise strategy.

---

[1] *The sample jigsaw instructions in this Appendix were adopted from material provided by Pierre Provost, physical education teacher at St. Pius XII School in Hull, Quebec.*

Bibliography

Adler, F. "The Rise of the Female Crook," *Psychology Today*, November, 1975.

Ajzen, I. and Fishbein, M. "Factors Influencing Intentions and the Intention-Behavior Relation," *Human Relations*, 27:1, 1974.

Albinson, J.G. and Andrew, G.M. (Eds.) *The Child and Sport and Physical Activity*, The Canadian Council on Children and Youth, 1407 Yonge Street, Toronto, 1976.

Alland, A. *The Human Imperative*, New York: Columbia University Press, 1972.

Arctic Sports: Rules and Regulations, Northwest Territories, Canarctic Publishing Ltd., 1973-74.

Aronson, E. *The Social Animal*, New York: W.H. Freeman Co., 1972.

Aronson, E. "The Jigsaw Route to Learning and Liking," *Psychology Today*, February, 1975.

Aronson, E., Blaney, N.T., Dehoney, J. and Rosa, J. "Interdependence in the Classroom," 1972, Cited in Aronson, E. *The Social Animal*, New York: W.H. Freeman, 1972.

Atkinson, J.W. and Raynor, J.O. *Motivation and Achievement*, Washington, D.C.: Winston and Sons, 1974.

Baker, T.K. and Ball. S.J. *Mass Media and Violence*, Washington, D.C.: U.S. Government Printing Office, Vol. IX, 1969.

Bandura, A. "What TV Violence Can Do to Your Child," *Look*, October 22, 16-52, 1963.

Bandura A. "Vicarious Processes: A Case of No-Trial Learning," In Berkowitz, L. *Advances in Experimental Social Psychology,* New York: Academic Press, Vol. 2, 1965.

Bandura, A. *Principles of Behaviour Modification,* Toronto: Holt, Rinehart and Winston, 1969.

Bandura, A., Rose, D. and Rose, A. "Imitation of Film-Mediated Aggressive Models," *Journal of Applied Social Psychology,* 66:3-16, 1963.

Bender, R., Brown, T., Coker, T., Fink, L., Morehouse, M. and Sharken, D., "Curriculum Development for the Jigsaw Process," See *Grass Roots Jigsawing* (Aronson, 1974) in bibliography.

Berkowitz, L. *Aggression: A Social Psychological Analysis,* New York: McGraw-Hill, 1962.

Berkowitz, L. "Concepts of Aggressive Drive: Some Additional Considerations," In Berkowitz, L. *Advances in Experimental Social Psychology,* New York: Academic Press, Vol. 2, 1965.

Berkowitz, L. "Aggression," *International Encyclopedia of the Social Sciences,* 1:168-174, 1968.

Berkowitz, L. *Roots of Aggression,* New York: Atherton, 1969.

Berkowitz, L., Corwin, R. and Hieronimus, R. "Film Violence and Subsequent Aggressive Tendencies," *Public Opinion Quarterly,* 27:217-229, 1963.

Berkowitz, L. "Sports, Competition and Aggression," Proceedings of the Fourth Canadian Symposium on Psycho-Motor Learning and Sport Psychology, University of Waterloo, Ontario, October, 1972.

Birkenshaw, L. "Communicating with Children Through Music," Orff Music Consultant Handout, Toronto Board of Education, 1976.

Birket-Smith, K. "Ethnographical Collections from the Northwest Passage," *Report of the 5th Thule Expedition, 1921-24,* 15 and 16: 1,2 Copenhagen: Gyldeddalske Boghandel, Nordisk for Lag, 1945.

Blaney, N.T., Stephan, C., Rosenfield, D., Aronson, E. and Sikes, J. "Interdependence in the Classroom: A Field Study and Replication," Unpublished Manuscript, University of Texas at Austin, 1975.

Blau, P.M. "Cooperation and Competition in a Bureaucracy," *American Journal of Sociology,* 59:530-35, 1954.

Boas, F. *The Central Eskimo,* Lincoln: University of Nebraska Press, 1964.

Boslooper, T. and Hayes M. *The Femininity Game,* New York: Stein and Day, 1973.

Botterill, C. "Democratic Behavior Modification as a Leadership Technique," Paper presented at the 6th Canadian Psychomotor Learning and Sport Psychology Symposium, Quebec City, October, 1975.

Botterill, C. "Leadership: How Every Kid Can Win," Paper presented at the 15th Annual Conference of the Alberta Teachers Association Health and Physical Education Council, Banff, Alberta, April, 1976.

Bouet, M. and Orlick, T.D. "The Meaning and Significance of Fun in Competitive Sport and Industrial Society," Proceedings of Eighth World Congress of Sociology, Toronto, August, 1974.

Bronfenbrenner, U. *Two Worlds of Childhood,* New York: Russell Sage Foundation, 1970.

Bruemmer, F. "Games Inuit Play," *North/Nord Magazine,* 17, 32-39, 1970.

Bruner, J.S. "Play is Serious Business," *Psychology Today,* January, 1975.

Bryan, J. and Schwartz, T. "Effects of Film Material Upon Childrens' Behavior," *Psychological Bulletin,* 75: 50-59, 1971.

Bryan, J.H. and Walbek, N.B. "Preaching and Practicing Generosity: Children's Actions and Reactions," *Child Development,* 41:253-329, 1970.

Buchanan, E.A. and Hanson, D.S. "Free Expression Through Movement," In *Humanistic Education Source Book,* (Eds. D.A. Read and S.B. Simon), Englewood Cliffs, New Jersy: Prentice Hall, 1975.

Bugliosi, V. and Gentry, C. *Helter Skelter: The True Story of the Manson Murders,* New York: Bantam Books, 1975.

Burgess, A.C. "Physical Activity in Middle-Aged Men: Incentives for Participation or Avoidance," Master's Thesis, University of Alberta, 1973.

Burns, J. "Chinese Bumpers Surprise Thunderbirds," *Toronto Globe and Mail*, Sports, December 8, 1973.

Burridge, K.D.L. "A Tangu Game," *Man*, 57: 88-89, 1957.

The Canadian Alternate Celebration Catalogue, Lanark Hills Foundation, RR #4, Perth, Ontario, 1975.

Canfield, J. and Wells, H.C. *100 Ways to Enhance Self-Concept in the Classroom*, Englewood Cliffs, New Jersey: Prentice Hall, 1976.

China Marches Ahead, The Embassy of the Peoples Republic of China, Ottawa, Canada, 1975.

Chittenden, G.E. "An Experimental Study in Measuring and Modifying Assertive Behavior in Young Children," *Monographs of the Society for Research in Child Development*, 1:31, 1942.

Christy, P.R., Gelfand, D.M. and Hartmann, D.P. "Effects of Competition Induced Frustration on Two Classes of Modeled Behaviour," *Developmental Psychology*, 5:104-111, 1971.

Church, R.M. "Applications of Behavior Theory to Social Psychology: Imitation and Competition," *In Social Facilitation and Imitative Behavior*, (Eds. E. Simmel, R. Hoppe and G. Milton), Boston: Allyn and Bacon, 1968.

Complo, J.M. *Dramakinetics in the Classroom*, Boston: Massy Plays Publishers Inc., 1974.

Coopersmith, S. *The Antecedents of Self-Esteem*, San Francisco: W.H. Freeman, 1967.

Cratty, B.J. *Learning About Human Behavior Through Active Games*, Englewood Cliffs, New Jersy: Prentice Hall, 1975.

Crime Statistics, Dominion Bureau of Statistics, Health and Welfare Division, Judicial Section, Ministry of Industry, Trade and Commerce, Ottawa, 1962-1974.

Crockenberg, S., Bryant, B. and Wilee, L.S. "The Effects of Cooperatively and Competitively Structured Learning Environments on Intrapersonal Behavior," Paper presented at the Annual Meeting of the American Psychological Association, New Orleans, September, 1974.

Crowinshield, E. *New Songs and Games*, Boston, Mass: The Boston Music Co., 1941.

Dauer, V.P. and Pangrazi, R.P. *Dynamic Physical Education for Elementary School Children,* Minneapolis: Burgess Publishing Company, 1975.

Davis, A.K. *A Northern Dilemma,* Bellingham, Wa.: Western Washington State College Press, 1967.

Davis, D.H. "The Balance Beam—A Bridge to Cooperation," *Teaching Exceptional Children,* Spring, 94-95, 1975.

Davis, G.A., Helfert, C.J. and Shapiro, G.R. "Let's Be an Ice Cream Machine—Creative Dramatics," *Humanistic Education Sourcebook,* (Eds. D.A. Read and S.B. Simon), Englewood Cliffs, New Jersey: Prentice Hall, 1975.

Deacove, J. *Cooperative Games: For Indoors and Out,* Family Pastimes, RR#4, Perth, Ontario, 1974.

DeKoven, B. "Creating the Play Community," In *The New Games Book* (Ed. A. Fluegelman), Garden City, N.Y.: Doubleday, 1976.

Deutsch, M. "An Experimental Study of the Effects of Cooperation and Competition Upon Group Process," *Human Relations,* 2:199-231, 1949.

Deutsch, M. "Cooperation and Trust: Some Theoretical Notes," Nebraska Symposium on Motivation (Ed. M.R. Jones), University of Nebraska Press, Lincoln, Nebraska, 1962.

DeVries, D.L. and Mescon, I. "Using TGT at the Moses DeWitt Elementary School: A Preliminary Report," Center for Social Organization of Schools, Johns Hopkins University, 1974.

Diebel, L. "Fight For Ancient Ways," *The Montreal Gazette,* October 18, 1975.

Doob, A. and Climie, R. "Delay of Measurement and the Effects of Film Violence," *Journal of Applied Social Psychology,* 8:36-142, 1972.

Doyle, P.H. "The Differential Effects of Multiple and Single Niche Play Activities on Interpersonal Relations Among Pre-Schoolers," (Eds. Lancy, D.F. and Tindall, B.A.) *The Anthropological Study of Play,* Cornwall, N.Y.: Leisure Press, 1976.

Dunn, G. "Effects of Win-Loss Ratio on Performance, Arousal and Satisfaction," Master's Thesis, Dept. of Kinanthropology, University of Ottawa, 1977.

Dunn, L.C. and Goldmen, H. "Competition and Noncompetition in Relation to Satisfaction and Feelings Toward Group and Nongroup Members," *Journal of Social Psychology*, 68:299-311, 1966.

Eastwood, J.M. "The Effects of Viewing a Film of Professional Hockey on Aggression," *Medicine and Science in Sports*, 6:2, 158-163, 1974.

Eaton, J. and Weil, R. *Culture and Mental Disorders*, New York: Free Press, 1955.

Eron, L., Huesmann, L., Lefkowitz, M. and Walder, L. "Does Television Violence Cause Aggression?" *American Psychologist*, 27:253-263, 1972.

Family Pastimes: Makers and Distributers of Games and Cooperation, Sales Catalogue #5, RR #4, Perth, Ontario, November, 1975.

Feshbach, S. "Dynamics and Morality of Violence and Aggression: Some Psychological Considerations," *American Psychologist*, 26:281-292, 1971.

Feshbach, N. and Feshbach, S. "The Relationship Between Empathy and Aggression in Two Age Groups," *Developmental Psychology*, 1:102-107, 1969.

Fishbein, M. and Ajzen, I. "Attitudes and Opinions," *Annual Review of Psychology*, Vol. 23, 1972.

Fluegelman, A. (Ed.) *The New Games Book*, Garden City, N.Y.: Doubleday, 1976.

Foley, C. and Yeomans, P. "Pilot Study Towards the Creation of Cooperative Physical Activities for Elementary School Children," Unpublished research project, University of Ottawa, 1975.

Friedrich, O. *Going Crazy*, New York: Avon Books, 1977.

Fromm, E. *The Anatomy of Human Destructiveness*, New York: Holt, Rinehart and Winston, 1973.

Galston, A.W. *Daily Life in People's China*, New York: Thomas Y. Crowell Company, 1973.

"Games People Play—Just for Fun", *National Geographic World*, August, 1976.

Glass, D.C. "Stress, Competition and Heart Attacks," *Psychology Today,* December, 1976.

Glassford, R.G. "An Application of a Theory of Games to the Transitional Eskimo Culture," Doctoral Dissertation, University of Illinois, Urbana-Champaign, 1970.

Glassford, R.G., Scott, H.A., Orlick, T.D., Bennington,E. and Adams, D. "Territorial Experimental Ski Training Program: Research Results," Paper presented at the 20th Biennial CAHPER Convention, Calgary, July, 1973.

Glassford, R.G. and Clumpner, R. "Physical Culture Inside the Peoples' Republic of China," Unpublished paper, Department of Physical Education, University of Alberta, 1974.

Goffman, E. *Encounters,* Indianapolis: Bobbs-Merrill, 1961.

Goldman, I. "The Bathonga of South Africa," In *Cooperation and Competition Among Primitive Peoples,* (Ed. M. Mead), Boston: Beacon Press, 1961.

Goldstein, J. and Arms, R. "Effects of Observing Athletic Contests on Hostility," *Sociometry,* 34:83-90, 1971.

Gardner, W.I. *Children with Learning and Behavior Problems: A Behavior Management Approach,* Boston: Allyn and Bacon, 1974.

Geen, R.G. and O'Neel, E.C. "Activation of Cue-Elicited Aggression by General Arousal," *Journal of Personality and Social Psychology,* 11:289-292, 1969.

Gelfand, D.M. and Hartman, D.P. "Some Detrimental Effects of Competitive Sports on Children's Behavior," Paper presented at the AMA Conference on the Mental Health Aspects of Sport, Atlantic City, New Jersey, June, 1975.

Gilbert, B. "Play," *Sports Illustrated,* October 13, 1975.

Gilder, W. *Schwatka's Search,* New York: Abercrombie and Fitch, 1966.

Ginsburg, H. and Opper S. *Piaget's Theory of Intellectual Development,* Englewoods Cliffs, New Jersey: Prentice Hall, 1969.

Goranson, R.E. "Media Violence and Aggressive Behavior: A Review of Experimental Research," In Berkowitz, L. *Advances in Experimental Social Psychology,* New York: Academic Press, Vol. 5, 1970.

Gorney, R. *The Human Agenda,* New York: Simon and Schuster, 1972.

Gorney, R. "Human Aggression," Paper presented at the AMA Conference on the Mental Health Aspects of Sports, Atlantic City, New Jersey, June, 1975.

Grass Roots Jigsawing, Interdependent Cooperative Learning Handbook written by students of E. Aronson, Kresge College, University of California, Santa Cruz, 1975.

Greenberg, P.T. "Competition in Children: An Experimental Study," *American Journal of Psychology,* 44: 221-248, 1932.

Haines, D.B. and Mckeachie, W.I. "Cooperative Versus Competitive Discussion Methods in Teaching Introductory Psychology," *Journal of Educational Psychology,* 58:386-90, 1967.

Hall, R.V. *Managing Behavior I: The Measurement of Behavior,* Lawrence, Kansas: H&H Enterprises, 1974.

Hanratty, M., O'Neal, E. and Sulzer, J., "Effects of Frustration Upon Imitation of Aggression," *Journal of Personality and Social Psychology,* 21: 3034, 1972.

Hansen, H. "Canadian Youth Are Hockey Has Beens by Fifteen Years of Age," *Canadian Journal of Health, Physical Education and Recreation,* January/February, 1970.

Hansen, H. *An Alternative to Minor Hockey in Canada,* School of Physical Education: University of Ottawa, December, 1974.

Harrison, M. and The Nonviolence and Children Program. "Season Openers: Games For More Than The Fun Of It," *Learning*—The Magazine For Creative Teaching, 5:1:64-68, August/September, 1976.

Harrison, M. and The Nonviolence and Children Program. *For the Fun of It: Selected Co-operative Games for Children and Adults,* Nonviolence and Children Program, Friends Peace Committee, 1515 Cherry Street, Philadelphia, Pa., 1976.

Harrington, R. *The Face of the Arctic,* New York: Henry Schuman, 1952.

Hart, B.M., Reynolds, N.J. and Baer, D.M "Effects of Contingent and Non-Contingent Social Reinforcement on the Cooperative

Play of a Pre-School Child," *Journal of Applied Behaviour Analysis*, 1:73-76, 1968.

Hart, M. *Kulila on Aboriginal Education*, Sydney: Australian and New Zealand Book Company, 1974.

Hartman, N. *Ethics: Moral Values*, New York: MacMillan, 1932.

Havemann, E. "Down Will Come Baby, Cycle and All," *Sports Illustrated*, August 13. 1973.

Havinghurst, R. "Play and Sports in the Maturation of Youth," Paper presented at the AMA Conference on the Mental Health Aspects of Sports, Atlantic City, New Jersey, June, 1975.

Hermon, S. "Contest and Rivalry—A Model of Competitive Behaviour," Proceedings of The Third World Congress on Sport Psychology, Madrid, June, 1973.

Hicks, D. "Imitation and Retention of Film-Mediated Aggressive Peer and Adult Models," *Journal of Personality and Social Psychology*, 2:97-100, 1965.

Hilyard, I. and Valla, V. *Making Music Your Own*, Morristown, New Jersey: Silver Burdett Company, 1971.

Holloway, S.M. and Hornstein, H.A. "How Good News Makes Us Good," *Psychology Today*, December, 1976.

Hopkins, P. "A Child's Model for Adult Games," Unpublished paper, Department of Athletics, University of Waterloo, Waterloo, Ontario, 1975.

Hsieh, C.K. and Yueh, H. *Hello! Hello! Are You There*, Foreign Languages Press, China Publications Center, P.O. Box 399, Peking, 1965.

Hubbard, L.R. *The Applied Scholastics Basic Study Manual*, Los Angeles: Applied Scholastics, Inc., 1972.

Hutton, S.K. *Among the Eskimos of Labrador*. Toronto: Musson Book Company, 1912.

Hyland, S.K. "Physical Activity: What Makes It Fun for 5 and 6 Year Old Children," Unpublished project, Department of Kinanthropology, University of Ottawa, 1974.

Hyland, H.J. and Orlick, T.D. "Physical Education Drop Outs:

Some Related Factors," Special Psycho-Motor Learning—Sports Psychology Issue of *Mouvement*, October, 1975.

Jenness, D. "The Life of the Cooper Eskimo," *Report of the Canadian Arctic Expedition, 1913-1918,* Vol. 12, Ottawa: Kings Printer, 1922.

Johnson, D.W. "Cooperativeness and Social Perspective Taking," *Journal of Personality and Social Psychology,* (in press), Cited in Johnson and Johnson, 1975.

Johnson, D.W. and Johnson, R.T. *Learning Together and Alone: Cooperation, Competition and Individualization,* Englewood Cliffs, New Jersey: Prentice Hall, 1975.

Johnson, R.N. *Aggression in Man and Animals,* Toronto: W.B. Saunders Company, 1972.

Johnson, R.T., Johnson, D.W. and Bryant, B. "Cooperation and Competition in the Classroom," *Elementary School Journal,* 74:3, 172-181, December, 1973.

Jones, E.E., Kanouse, D.E., Kelley, H.H., Nisbett, R.E., Valins, S. and Weiner, B. *Attribution: Perceiving the Causes of Behavior,* Morristown, New Jersey: General Learning Press, 1972.

Jones, R.F. "Toting up the Butcher's Bill," *Sports Illustrated,* November 8, 1976.

Kagan, S., and Madsen, M.C. "Cooperation and Competition of Mexican, Mexican-American, and Anglo-American Children of Two Ages Under Four Instructional Sets," *Developmental Psychology,* 5, 1:32-39, 1971.

Kane, J.E. "Personality, Body Concept and Performance," In *Psychological Aspects of Physical Education and Sport,* (Ed. J.E. Kane), London: Routledge and Kegan Paul, 1972.

Kaufmann, H. *Aggression and Altruism,* New York: Holt, Rinehart and Winston, 1970.

Kiesler, C. *The Psychology of Commitment,* New York: Academic Press, 1971.

Kirby, F.D. and Toler, H.C. "Modification of Pre-School Isolate Behaviour: A Case Study," *Journal of Applied Behaviour Analysis,* 4:309-314, 1970.

Kome, P. "Fun and Games," *The Canadian Magazine,* December 25, 1976.

Kome, P. "Cooperative Games," *Homemaker's Magazine,* 11:5:78-86, September, 1976.

Kramer, J. *Lombardi: Winning Is The Only Thing,* Simon and Schuster of Canada, Pocket Books, 1971.

Kranidiotis, P.T. "On the Therapeutic Value and the Psychological Mechanisms of Defense in Sport Activities of Neurotic Patients," Proceedings of the Third World Congress on Sport Psychology, Madrid, June, 1973.

Kropst K.P. *Mutual Aid,* New York: Doubleday, 1902.

Labouisse, H.R. *The State of Children and UNICEF,* UNICEF Headquarters, United Nations, New York, 1975.

Labow, J. "Fun Program Smash Hit—Waterloo Intramural Director in Dilemma," *The Toronto Globe and Mail,* February 8, 1977.

Laing, R.D. and Esterson, A. *Sanity, Madness and the Family,* Baltimore: Penguin Books, 1970.

Lamblin, B. *My Skin Barely Covers Me,* Uncle John's Sports Art Publication. 24498 Meadow Lane, Perris, California.

Larson, D.L. and Spreitzer, E. "A Social Perspective of Youth Sports Involvement and Parental Involvement," Paper presented at the Popular Culture Association Convention, Milwaukee, Wisconsin, May, 1974.

Lavergne, B.D. and Mercantini, P.L. "Socialization and Learning Through Cooperative Games," Unpublished research paper, University of Ottawa, April, 1976.

Le Boulch, J. *L'Education par le Mouvement,* Paris: Les Editions Sociales Francaise, 1968.

Leith, L.M. "Filmed Sport Models and Aggressive Predispositions in the Young Audience," Master's Thesis, University of Western Ontario, 1973.

Leith, L.M. and Orlick, T.D. "The Effect of Viewing Aggressive and Non-Aggressive Sport Models on the Aggressive

Presidpositions of the Young Audience," Proceedings of the Third World Congress on Sport Psychology, Madrid, June, 1973.

Leith, L. and Orlick T.D. "An Analysis of Aggressive Predispositions in Young Hockey Players at Three Different Competitive Levels," Unpublished study, 1974.

Lentz, T.F. *Towards a Science of Peace,* Peace Research Laboratory, 6251 San Bonita, St. Louis, Missouri, 1955.

Lentz, T.F. and Cornelius, R. *All Together—A Manual of Cooperative Games,* Peace Research Laboratory, 6251 San Bonita, St. Louis, Missouri, 1950.

Leonard, G.B. "Winning Isn't Everything: It's Nothing," *Intellectual Digest,* October, 45-47, 1973.

Leonard, G.B. "The Games People Should Play," *Esquire,* October, 1974.

Lepper, M.R., Greene D. and Nisbett, R.E. "Undermining Children's Intrinsic Interest with Extrinsic Reward," *Journal of Personality and Social Psychology,* 28:129-137, 1973.

Letheren, C.A. "Role of the Coach," Canadian Coaching Development Program, Phase II, 1975.

Lever, J. "Soccer: Opium of the Brazilian People," *Trans-Action,* 7:36-43, 1969.

Liebert, R.M., Neale, J.M. and Davidson, E.S. *The Early Window: Effects of Television on Children and Youth,* New York: Pergamon Press, 1973.

Lofland, J. *Analyzing Social Settings,* Belmont, Cal.: Wadsworth Publishing Company, 1971.

Lovass, O. "Effect of Exposure to Symbolic Aggression on Aggressive Behavior," *Child Devlopment,* 32: 37-44, 1961.

Lucker, G.W., Rosenfield, D., Sikes, J. and Aronson, E. "The Interdependent Classroom: A Technique for Improving Minority Performance," *Journal of Educational Psychology,* (Submitted for Publication).

Ludwig, J. *Games of Fear and Winning,* Toronto: Doubleday of Canada, 1975.

Lunde, D.T. "Our Murder Boom," *Psychology Today*, July, 1975.

MacFarlan, A.A. *Book of American Indian Games*, New York: Association Press, 1958.

Maclaine, S. *You Can Get There From Here*, New York: W.W. Norton and Company, 1975.

Madsen, C.A. "Rules, Praise and Ignoring—Elements of Elementary Classroom Control," In *Operant Conditioning in the Classroom*, (Ed. C.E. Pitts), New York: Crowell Company, 1971.

Martens, R. *Social Psychology and Physical Activity*, New York: Harper and Row, 1975.

Martens, R. "Kid Sports: A Den of Iniquity or Land of Promise," Address given at the National College of Physical Education Association Men Conference, Hot Springs, Arkansas, January, 1976.

Maslow, A.H. *Motivation and Personality*, New York: Harper and Row, 1970.

Mauldon, E. and Redfern, H.B. *Games Teaching—A New Approach for the Primary School*, London: Macdonald and Evans, 1969.

McCandless, B.R. and Evans, E.D. *Children and Youth: Psychosocial Development*, Hinsdale, Illinois: Dryden Press, 1973.

McClintock, C.C. and Nuttin, J.M. "Development of Competitive Behavior in Children Across Two Cultures," *Journal of Experimental Social Psychology*, 5:203-218, 1969.

McFarland, C. (Ed.). *Canada 1973*, Year Book Division, Statistics Canada, Ministry of Industry, Trade and Commerce, Ottawa, 1973.

McGuire, J.M. and Thomas, M.H. "Effects of Sex, Competence, and Competition on Sharing Behavior in Children," *Journal of Personality and Social Psychology*, 32, 3:490-494, 1975.

McMurtry, W.R. "Investigation and Inquiry into Violence in Amateur Hockey," Report to the Ontario Minister of Community and Social Services, Ontario Government Bookstore, Toronto, 1974.

McNally, J.F. "Factors Limiting Sports Participation by High School Females and Males," Master's Thesis, Department of

Kinanthropology, University of Ottawa, 1976.

McNally, J.F. and Orlick, T.D. "Cooperative Sports Structures. A Preliminary Analysis," Special Psycho-Motor Learning—Sports Psychology Issue of *Mouvement*, October, 1975.

MD Medical Newsmagazine, "Spotlight on Sports—Problems in Competitive Athletics and New Approaches to Physical Education," 19:9:45-52, 1975.

Mead, M. "The Arapesh of New Guinea," In *Cooperation and Competition Among Primitive Peoples*, (Ed. M. Mead), Boston: Beacon Press, 1961.

Meggyesy, D. *Out of their League,* New York: Ramparts Press, 1971.

Meichenbaum, D.H., Bowers, K.S. and Ross, R.R. "A Behavioural Analysis of Teacher Expectancy Effect," *Journal of Personality and Social Psychology*, 13:306-316, 1969.

Merriam, E. "We're Teaching Our Children That Violence Is Fun," *The Ladies Home Journal,* October, 1964.

Meyer, T. "Effects of Viewing Justified and Unjustified Real Film Violence on Aggressive Behavior," *Journal of Personality and Social Psychology*, 23:19-21, 1972.

Milby, J.B., Jr. "Modification of Extreme Social Isolation by Contingent Social Reinforcement," *Journal of Applied Behaviour Analysis*, 2:149-152, 1970.

Millar, F. *"Review on Every Kid Can Win,"* Today's Education (NEA Journal), September/October, 1975.

Mitchell, I.S. "Aboriginal Education," *The Aboriginal Child at School*, 1: 4: 21-30, December, 1973.

Mirsky, J. "The Eskimo of Greenland," *In Cooperation and Competition Among Primitive Peoples*, (Ed. M. Mead), Boston: Beacon Press, 1961.

Moncrieff, J. "Physical Games and Amusements of the Australian Aboriginal," *Australian Journal of Physical Education*, 36:5-11, 1966.

Montagu, A. *On Being Human,* New York: Hawthorn Books, 1966.

Montagu, A. (Ed.) *Man and Aggression,* New York: Oxford University Press, 1968.

Montagu, A. *The Nature of Human Aggression*, New York: Oxford University Press, 1976.

Moriarty, D. and Guilmette, A. M. "Sport Institute for Research: Change Agent Research (SIR/CAR)," Paper presented at 79th Annual Meeting of the National College Physical Education Association for Men, Hot Springs, Arkansas, January, 1976.

Moriarty, D. and Duthic, J. "Sports Institute for Research: Change Agent Research," Faculty of Physical and Health Education, University of Windsor, Windsor, Ontario, 1975.

Morris, G.S.D. *How to Change the Games Children Play*, Minneapolis: Burgess Publishing Company, 1976.

Morris, R.J. and Dolker, M. "Developing Cooperative Play in Socially Withdrawn Retarded Children," *Mental Retardation*, 12:6:24-27, 1974.

Mountford, C.P. *Brown Men and Red Sand*, Sydney: Angus and Robertson Ltd., 1964.

Mulvoy, M. "Hockey is Courting Disaster," *Sports Illustrated*, January 27, 1975.

Murphy, G., Murphy, L. and Newcomb, T.H. *Experimental Social Psychology*, New York: Harper, 1937.

Mussen, P. and Rutherford, E. "Effects of Aggressive Cartoons on Childrens' Aggressive Play," *Journal of Applied Social Psychology*, 62:461-464, 1961.

Nance, J. *The Gentle Tasaday*, New York: Harcourt Brace Jovanovich, 1975.

National Conference of Program Planning in Games and Sports for Boys and Girls of Elementary School Age, Report distributed by the California State Department of Education, May, 1953.

Nebiolo, G. and Wilkinson, E. *The People's Comic Book*, Garden City, N.Y.: Doubleday and Company, 1973.

Nelson, J.D., Gelfand, D.M. and Hartmann, D.P. "Children's Aggression Following Competition and Exposure to Aggressive Models," *Child Development*, 40:1085-1097, 1969.

Nelson, L.L. and Kagan, S. "Competition the Star-Spangled Scramble," *Psychology Today*, September, 1972.

New Games Newsletter, 2:1, Summer 1976, P.O. Box 7901, San Francisco, California.

New, P.K. "Barefoot Doctors and Health Care in the Peoples' Republic of China," Unpublished paper, Department of Behavioral Science, Faculty of Medicine, University of Toronto, 1973.

Newcomer, B.L. and Morrison, T.L. "Play Therapy with Institutionalized Mentally Retarded Children," *American Journal of Mental Deficiency*, 78: 6: 727-733, May 1974.

Nissen, H. "Social Behavior in Primates," In *Comparative Psychology*, (Ed. C.P. Stone), Englewood Cliffs, New Jersey: Prentice Hall, 1951.

Northern Environment Foundation Poster, Box 1409, Winnipeg, Manitoba.

Northern Games, Official Programs and Reports, Northern Games Association, Box 1184, Inuvik, Northwest Territories, 1970-1976.

Nuligak, R., *I Nuligak*, Richmond Hill, Ontario: Simon and Schuster Pocket Book, 1971.

O'Connor, R.D. "Modification of Social Withdrawal Through Symbolic Modeling," *Journal of Applied Behaviour Analysis*, Summer, 1969.

Offir, C.W. "Don't Take It Lying Down," *Psychology Today*, January, 1975.

Ogilvie, B.C. and Tutko, T.A. "Sport: If You Want to Build Character, Try Something Else," *Psychology Today*, October, 1971.

Olson, R. "A Manual of Cooperative Games," *Co Evolution Quarterly*, Summer, 1976. (Box 428, Sausalito, Calif.).

Orlick, E. and Mosley, J. *Teacher's Illustrated Handbook of Stunts*, Englewood Cliffs, New Jersey: Prentice Hall, 1963.

Orlick, T.D., "A Socio-Psychological Analysis of Early Sports Participation," Doctoral Dissertation, University of Alberta, 1972.

Orlick, T.D. "Sport in China—Friendship First, Competition

Second," *Canadian Journal of Health, Physical Education and Recreation,* January/February, 1973.

Orlick, T.D. "Children's Sport A Revolution is Coming," *Canadian Journal of Health, Physical Education and Recreation,* January/February, 1973.

Orlick, T.D. "An Analysis of Expectancy as a Motivational Factor Influencing Sports Participation," Proceedings of Third World Congress on Sport Psychology, Madrid, Spain, June, 1973.

Orlick, T.D. "Sports Participation—A Process of Shaping Behavior," *Human Factors,* 5:16, October 1974.

Orlick, T.D. "The Athletic Drop Out—A High Price for Inefficiency," *Canadian Journal of Health, Physical Education and Recreation,* November / December, 1974.

Orlick, T.D. "Questionnaire Results," In *An Alternative to Minor Hockey in Canada,* (H. Hansen), School of Physical Education, University of Ottawa, December, 1974.

Orlick, T.D. "Hockey Coach on the Right Track," Unpublished community report on results of Stittsville hockey study, University of Ottawa, March, 1975.

Orlick, T.D. "The Sports Environment: A Capacity to Enhance— A Capacity to Destroy", In *The Status of Psychomotor Learning and Sport Psychology Research,* (Ed. B.S. Rushall), Dartmouth, Nova Scotia: Sport Science Associates, 1975.

Orlick, T. and Botterill, C. *Every Kid Can Win,* Chicago: Nelson Hall Publishers, 1975. (325 W. Jackson Blvd).

Orlick, T.D., Partington, J.T., Scott, H.A. and Glassford, R.G. "The Development of the Skimetric Differential: A Childranistic Approach," Special Psycho-Motor Learning— Sports Psychology Issues of *Mouvement,* October, 1975.

Orlick, T.D. "Psychological Circles in Gymnastics," In *The Advanced Study of Gymnastics* (Ed. J. Salmela), Springfield, Illinois: C.C. Thomas Company, 1976.

Orlick, T.D. "Games of Acceptance and Psycho-Social Adjustment," in *The Humanistic and Mental Health Aspects of Sports, Exercise and Recreation,* (Ed. T. Craig), American Medical Association, 1976.

Orlick, T.D. and Foley, C. "Pre-School Cooperative Games: A Preliminary Perspective," Proceedings of the Ninth Canadian Symposium on Psycho-Motor Learning and Sports Psychology, (Ed. B.A. Kerr), University of Calgary, Calgary, Alberta, Sept., 1977.

Orlick, T.D. "Cooperative Games: Systematic Analysis and Cooperative Impact," In *Psychological Perspectives in Youth Sports*, (Eds. F. Smoll and R. Smith), Washington, D.C.: Hemisphere Publishers, 1978.

Orlick, T.D. *The Cooperative Sports and Games Book*, New York: Pantheon Books, 1978.

The Ottawa Journal. "Survival Hinges on Love—Trudeau," June 1, 1976.

The Ottawa Journal. "Turn Words of Love into Action, PM Told," June, 1, 1976.

Paloutzian, R.F. "Promotion of Positive Social Interaction in Severely Retarded Children," *American Journal of Mental Deficiency*, 75: 4: 519-524, 1971.

"Pressureless Sports,"*Parade Magazine*, January 11, 1976.

Partington, J.T., Orlick, T.D. and Scott, H.A. "Effects of the Territorial Experimental Ski Training Program in Tulita, N.W.T.," Special Psycho-Motor Learning—Sports Psychology Issue of *Mouvement*, October, 1975.

Paul, J. and Laulicht, J. *In Your Opinion*, Canadian Peace Research Institute, Clarkson, Ontario, 1963.

Pearce, T. "The Games Eskimos Play," *Canadian Panorama*, April 11, 1970. (Reprinted in Northern Games Program, 1971).

Piaget, J. and Barbel, I. *The Psychology of The Child*, New York: Basic Books, 1969.

Pierce, C.H. "Behaviour Modification and Motor Development," Proceedings from the Fourth Canadian Symposium on Psycho-Motor Learning and Sports Psychology, University of Waterloo, October, 1972.

Pitts, C.E. (Ed.), *Operant Conditioning in the Classroom*, New York: T. Y. Crowell Company, 1971.

Porter, K. "Dialogue with Swimmers: Age Group Drop Outs," *Swimming World*, 13:56, 1972.

Quilitch, R.H. and Risley, T.R. "The Effects of Play Materials on Social Play," *Journal of Applied Behaviour Analysis*, 4:573-578, 1973.

Rabkin, B. "Growing Up Dead," *Homemaker's Magazine*, 11:4:46-58, July, 1976.

Ralbousky M. "But Who Is Larry Csonka," *Sport*, March, 1972.

Rasmussen, K. "The Netsilik Eskimos," *Report of the 5th Thule Expedition, 1921-24"* 8:1, 2, Copenhagen: Gyldeddalske Boghandel, Nordisk Forlag, 1931.

Rausch, H.L. "Interaction Sequences," *Journal of Personality and Social Psychology*, 2:487-499, 1965.

Rausch, H.L. Dittmann, A.T. and Taylor, T.I. "Person, Setting, and Change in Social Interaction," *Human Relations*, 12:361-379, 1959.

Rausch, H.L., Farhman, I. and Llewellyn, L.G. "Person, Setting and Change in Social Interaction: II, A Normal Control Study," *Human Relations*, 13:305-333, 1960.

Read, D.A. "The Influence of Competitive and Non-Competitive Programs of Physical Education on Body Image and Self-Concept," Annual Proceedings of NCPEAM, AAHPER, Washington, 1969.

Read, D.A. and Simon S.B., *Humanistic Education Sourcebook*, Englewood Cliffs, New Jersey: Prentice Hall, 1975.

Reed, W.F. "An Ugly Affair in Minneapolis," *Sports Illustrated*, February 7, 1972.

Reider, H. *Sport as Therapy*, Berlin, Frankfurt, Munchen: Bartels and Wernitz, 1971.

Richmond, B.O. and Vance, J.J. "Cooperative-Competitive Game Strategy and Personality Characteristics of Black and of White Children," *Interpersonal Development*, 5:2 78-85, 1974/75.

Risley, T. "The Social Context of Self Control," Paper presented at the Eighth Banff International Conference on Behavior Modification, Banff, Alberta, March, 1976.

Robertson, I "Sport and Play in Aboriginal Culture—Then and Now," Proceedings of the 7th National Biannual Conference of the Australian Council for Health, Physical Education and Recreation, Perth, Western Australia, January, 1975.

Robertson, J. "Food for Thought," *Hockey Review 1974-75,* Canadian Amateur Hockey Association, Ottawa, Ontario, 1975.

Robinson, J.P. and Shaver, P. *Measures of Psychological Attitudes,* Ann Arbor: Survey Research Center, 1969.

Rogers, V.M. and Goodloe, A.H. "Simulation Games as a Method," In *Humanistic Education Sourcebook,* (Eds. D.A. Read and S.B. Simon), Englewood Cliffs, New Jersey: Prentice Hall, 1975.

Rosenberg, M. *Society and the Adolescent Self-Image,* Princeton, New Jersey: Princeton University Press, 1965.

Rosenthal, R. and Jacobson, L. *Pygmalion in the Classroom.* New York: Holt, Rinehart and Winston, 1968.

Rosethal, R. and Jacobson, L. *The Pygmalion Effect: What You Expect Is What You Get.* Del Mar, Cal.: Ziff Davis Publishing Co., 1974.

Rushall, B.S. "Two Observational Scales for Sporting Environments," Paper presented at the Fifth Canadian Symposium on Sport Psychology, Montreal, October, 1973.

Rushall, B.S. "A Direction for Contemporary Sport Psychology." Address given at the First Canadian Multi-Disciplinary Congress for the Study of Sport, Montreal, October, 1973.

Russell, B. *The Conquest of Happiness,* New York: Bantam, 1958.

Ryan, E.D. "The Cathartic Effect of Vigorous Motor Activity on Aggressive Behavior," *Research Quarterly,* 41:543-554, 1970.

Ryan, E.D. "Reaction to Berkowitz's Paper," Proceedings of the Fourth Canadian Symposium on Psycho-Motor Learning and Sport Psychology, University of Waterloo, October, 1972.

Sanderson, J.D. "Kids' Football: Age and Youth and Namath," New York Times, Sunday, December 12, 1976.

Salter, M. "Games and Pastimes of the Australian Aboriginal," Master's Thesis, Department of Physical Education, University of Alberta, 1967.

Sax, S. and Hollander, S. *Reality Games*, New York: The MacMillan Co., 1972.

Scanlan, T.K. "The Effect of Success-Failure in the Perception of Threat in a Competitive Situation," *Research Quarterly*, (Submitted for publication).

Schurr, E.I. *Movement Experiences for Children: A Humanistic Approach to Elementary School Physical Education*, Second edition, Englewood Cliffs, New Jersey: Prentice Hall, 1975.

Schwartzman, H.B. "The Anthropological Study of Children's Play," *Annual Review of Anthropology*, 5: 289-328, 1976.

Scott, H. A. "Self, Coach and Team: A Theoretical and Empirical Application of the Social Interactionist Perspective to Teenage Sports Candidacy and Participation," Doctoral Dissertation, University of Alberta, Fall, 1973.

Scott, H.A. "Competitive Sport Outcome: Self-Fulfillment and Participation or Self-Destruction and Elimination," *Katimavik*, the University of Alberta, 1:1, Winter, 1974.

Scott, H.A., Glassford, R.G., Orlick, T.D. and Partington, J.T. "The Need for an Applied Socio-Psychology of Sport: An Assessment Based on Northern Experiences," Paper presented at the 7th Canadian Conference on Psycho-Motor Learning and Sport Psychology, Quebec City, Quebec, October, 1975.

Scott, J. *Aggression*, Chicago: Chicago University Press, 1958.

Selye, H. *Stress Without Distress*, New York: J.B. Lippincott Co., 1974.

Selkin, J. "Rape," *Psychology Today*, January, 1975.

Service, E.R. *The Hunters*, Englewood Cliffs, New Jersey: Prentice Hall, 1966.

Shaw, G. *Meat on the Hoof.* New York: Dell Publishing Company, 1972.

Sherif, C.W. and Rattray, G.D. "Psycho-Social Development and Activity in Middle Childhood," Paper presented at the First National Conference on the Child in Sport, Queen's University, Kingston, Ontario, May, 1973.

Sherif, M. "Experiments in Group Conflict," *Scientific American*, November, 1956.

Sherif, M., Harvey, O.J., White, B.J., Hood, W. and Sherif, C. *The Robbers Cave Experiment—Intergroup Conflict and Cooperation*, Norman: University of Oklahoma, 1971.

Sidel, R. *Women and Child Care In China*, New York: Penguin Books, 1973.

Simon, S.B., Leland, W.H. and Kirschenbaum, H. *Values Clarification: A Handbook of Practical Strategies for Teachers and Students*, New York: Hart Publishing Company, 1972.

Sipes, R.G. "Sports as a Control for Aggression," Paper presented at the American Medical Association Conference on the Mental Health Aspects of Sport, Atlantic City, New Jersey, June, 1975.

Skinner, B.F. *Beyond Freedom and Dignity*, New York: Alfred A. Knopf, 1971.

Slack, J. and Hiland, B. "The Effects of a Perceptual-Motor Program on the Development of Motor Skills and Social Interaction in the Atypical Child," Unpublished Research Paper, University of Ottawa, April, 1976.

Smith, M. D. "Parents, Peers, and Coach's Sanctions for Assaultive Behaviour in Hockey," Paper Presented at the Congress: Sport in the Modern World, Munich, Germany, August, 1972.

Smith, M.F.R. "A Preliminary Case for Classifying Sports Environments by Participant Objectives," *Canadian Journal of Health, Physical Education and Recreation*, September/October, 1974.

Smith, M.F.R. "Sport and Physical Activity as Possible Factors in the Child's Psychological and Social Development," *Canadian Journal of Health, Physical Education and Recreation*, May/June, 1976.

Smoll, F. and Smith, R. (Eds.) *Psychological Perspectives In Youth Sports*, Washington, D.C.: Hemisphere Publishers, 1978.

Snyder, E.E. "High School Athletes and Their Coaches: Educational Plans and Advice," *Sociology of Education*, 45:313-325, 1972.

Snyder, E.E. and Spreitzer, E.A. "Involvement in Sports and Psychological Well-Being," Proceedings of the Third World Congress on Sport Psychology, Madrid, June, 1973.

Sowada, A. "New Guinea's Fierce Asmat: A Heritage of

Headhunting," In *Vanishing Peoples of the Earth,* (Ed. R.L. Breeden), National Geographic Society, 1968.

Sports in China The People's Sports Publishing House, Peking: Foreign Languages Press, 1973.

Staples, I. "Outdoor Education and the Quality of Life: What the Children Think," *Canadian Journal of Health, Physical Education and Recreation,* March/April, 1977

Stefansson, V. "The Stefansson—Anderson Arctic Expedition, American Museum: Preliminary Ethnological Report 1914," *Anthropology Papers of the American Museum of Natural History,* 14:1, 1919.

Stendler, C., Damrin, D. and Haines, A. "Studies in Cooperation and Competition: 1. The Effects of Working for Group and Individual Rewards on the Social Climate of Children's Groups," *Journal of Genetic Psychology,* 79:173-79, 1951.

Taylor, A. "1976 Northern Games In Coppermine," *Inuvialuit 5,* 1976.

Tharpe, R.G. and Wetzel, R.J. *Behaviour Modification in the Natural Environment,* New York: Academic Press, 1969.

Tonkinson, R. *The Jigalong Mob: Aboriginal Victors of the Desert Crusade,* Menlo Park, Cal.: Cummings Publishing Company, 1974.

Trudeau, P.E. Inaugural address to Habitat, the U.N. Conference on Human Settlements, Vancouver, British Columbia, May 31, 1976.

Tseng, S.C. "An Experimental Study of the Effect of Three Types of Distribution of Reward Upon Work Efficiency and Group Dynamics," Doctoral Dissertation, Columbia University, 1969.

Tulita News, Collin Campbell School, Fort Norman, NWT, 1974-76.

Turner, C. and Berkowitz, L. "Identification with Film Aggressor (Covert Role Taking) and Reactions to Film Violence," *Journal of Personality and Social Psychology,* 21:256-264, 1972.

Turner, E. "The Effect of Viewing College Football, Basketball, and Wrestling on the Elicited Aggressive Responses of Male Spectators," *Contemporary Psychology of Sport,* Chicago: The Athletic Institute, 325-328, 1970.

Turner, L.M. "Ethnology of the Ungava District," *11th Annual*

Report of the Bureau of American Ethnology: Smithsonian Institute 1889-1890, Washingon, D.C.: Government Printing Office, 1894.

Underwood, J. "Taking the Fun Out of a Game," *Sports Illustrated,* November 17, 1975.

Vayer, P. "Physical Education as an Initial Way of Approaching Maladjusted Adolescents," Proceedings of the Third World Congress on Sport Psychology, Madrid, June, 1973.

Walters, R.H. and Brown, M. "Studies of Reinforcement of Aggression: III. Transfer of Responses to an Interpersonal Situation," *Child Development,* 34, 563-571, 1963.

Walters, R.H., Leat, M. and Mezei, L. "Inhibition and Disinhibition of Responses Through Empathetic Learning," *Canadian Journal of Psychology,* 17:235-243, 1963.

Walters, R.H. and Thomas, E.L. "Enhancement of Punitiveness by Visual and Audiovisual Displays," *Canadian Journal of Psychology,* 16:244-255, 1963.

Wankel, L.M. "Competition: It's Nature and Effects," Unpublished paper, University of Alberta, 1971.

Wankel, L.M. "The Effects of Awards on Competition," Paper presented to Kitchener-Waterloo Sports Council, January, 1974.

Wankel, L.M. "Psychological Considerations for Organizing Intramural Sport Programs," Address Given at the Geneva Park Conference on Intramural Sports, Geneva Park, Ontario, April, 1974.

Ward, B. "Children—An Endangered Species," Special Issue on the Child and the Environment, *UNICEF News,* 1:83:16-18, 1975.

Washburn, S.L. and Lancaster, C.S. "The Evolution of Hunting," In *Man, The Hunter,* (Eds. R.B. Lee and I. DeVore), Chicago: Aldine, 1968.

Way, B. *Development Through Drama,* London: Longman, 1967.

Wehman, P. "Establishing Play Behaviors in Mentally Retarded Youth," *Rehabilitation Literature,* 36:8:238-246, 1975.

Witt, J., Campbell, M. and Witt, P. *A Mannual of Therapeutic Group Activities for Leisure Education,* Department of Recreology, University of Ottawa, 1973.

Wright, J.E. Personal correspondance with Director of Parks and Recreation for the town of Grimsby, Ontario, 1975.

Yang, Y. and Liang K. *I Am on Duty Today,* Peking: Foreign Lanuage Press, 1966.

Zillman, D., Katcher, A.H. and Milevsky, B. "Excitation Transfer from Physical Exercise to Subsequent Aggressive Behavior," *Journal of Experimental Social Psychology,* 8:247-259, 1972.

Zimbardo, P.G., Pilkonis, P.A. and Norwood, R.M. "The Social Disease Called Shyness," *Psychology Today,* May, 1975.

Zuk, W. *Eskimo Games,* Curriculum Section, Education Division, Northern Administration Branch, Department of Indian Affairs and Northern Development, Ottawa, 1967.

Zuk, W. "Indian and Eskimo Games," *The New Trail,* April, 1969, (Reprinted in Northern Games Program, 1971).

Index